S. Hrg. 106-1072: The 1996 Campaign Finance Investigations

U.S. Government Printing Office (GPO)

The BiblioGov Project is an effort to expand awareness of the public documents and records of the U.S. Government via print publications. In broadening the public understanding of government and its work, an enlightened democracy can grow and prosper. Ranging from historic Congressional Bills to the most recent Budget of the United States Government, the BiblioGov Project spans a wealth of government information. These works are now made available through an environmentally friendly, print-on-demand basis, using only what is necessary to meet the required demands of an interested public. We invite you to learn of the records of the U.S. Government, heightening the knowledge and debate that can lead from such publications.

Included are the following Collections:

Budget of The United States Government
Presidential Documents
United States Code
Education Reports from ERIC
GAO Reports
History of Bills
House Rules and Manual
Public and Private Laws

Code of Federal Regulations
Congressional Documents
Economic Indicators
Federal Register
Government Manuals
House Journal
Privacy act Issuances
Statutes at Large

S. Hrg. 106–1072

THE 1996 CAMPAIGN FINANCE INVESTIGATIONS

HEARING

BEFORE THE

COMMITTEE ON THE JUDICIARY
UNITED STATES SENATE

ONE HUNDRED SIXTH CONGRESS

SECOND SESSION

———

JUNE 27, 2000

———

Serial No. J–106–93

———

Printed for the use of the Committee on the Judiciary

U.S. GOVERNMENT PRINTING OFFICE

75–237   WASHINGTON : 2001

For sale by the Superintendent of Documents, U.S. Government Printing Office
Internet: bookstore.gpo.gov Phone: toll free (866) 512–1800; DC area (202) 512–1800
Fax: (202) 512–2250 Mail: Stop SSOP, Washington, DC 20402–0001

COMMITTEE ON THE JUDICIARY

ORRIN G. HATCH, Utah, *Chairman*

STROM THURMOND, South Carolina
CHARLES E. GRASSLEY, Iowa
ARLEN SPECTER, Pennsylvania
JON KYL, Arizona
MIKE DeWINE, Ohio
JOHN ASHCROFT, Missouri
SPENCER ABRAHAM, Michigan
JEFF SESSIONS, Alabama
BOB SMITH, New Hampshire

PATRICK J. LEAHY, Vermont
EDWARD M. KENNEDY, Massachusetts
JOSEPH R. BIDEN, JR., Delaware
HERBERT KOHL, Wisconsin
DIANNE FEINSTEIN, California
RUSSELL D. FEINGOLD, Wisconsin
ROBERT G. TORRICELLI, New Jersey
CHARLES E. SCHUMER, New York

MANUS COONEY, *Chief Counsel and Staff Director*
BRUCE A. COHEN, *Minority Chief Counsel*

CONTENTS

STATEMENTS OF COMMITTEE MEMBERS

WITNESS

SUBMISSIONS FOR THE RECORD

THE 1996 CAMPAIGN FINANCE INVESTIGATIONS

TUESDAY, JUNE 27, 2000

U.S. SENATE,
COMMITTEE ON THE JUDICIARY,
Washington, DC.

The committee met, pursuant to notice, at 2:06 p.m., in room SH–216, Hart Senate Office Building, Hon. Orrin G. Hatch presiding.

Also present: Senators Specter, Leahy, Grassley, Thurmond, Feingold, Feinstein, Kyl, Torricelli, Schumer, Sessions, and Smith.

OPENING STATEMENT OF HON. ORRIN G. HATCH, A U.S. SENATOR FROM THE STATE OF UTAH

The CHAIRMAN. General, if you could raise your right hand. Do you solemnly swear to tell the truth, the whole truth, and nothing but the truth, so help you God?

Attorney General RENO. I do.

The CHAIRMAN. Thank you.

I am pleased to convene this hearing of the Judiciary Committee to continue its oversight of the Department of Justice.

I will shortly turn to Senator Specter who has been tasked by the committee to head up this effort. I have to commend Senator Specter for his hard work and diligence in pursuing this oversight project, often in the face of resistance from the administration and the Justice Department, and I am glad to have been able to facilitate his efforts to obtain the documents and information necessary to complete the work of this committee.

Finally, I would also like to welcome our Attorney General and thank her for her attendance here today.

The campaign finance abuses of the 1996 Presidential election were a low watermark in our political history. Public confidence in our institutions and system of justice has been severely undermined. Vigorous and timely enforcement of our election laws would have gone a long way towards restoring the public's faith. Unfortunately, the Justice Department, through its many stops and starts, has failed to accomplish this goal, and we now find ourselves on the threshold of a new election with many old questions that remain unanswered.

I have made no secret of my strongly held view that an independent counsel for campaign finance-related matters should have been appointed long ago. The committee was the first to formally request the appointment of an independent counsel to investigate these matters. The work of this committee revealed that many others inside the Justice Department felt exactly the same way. FBI Director Freeh, Charles La Bella, Robert Litt, and now the current head of the Campaign Task Force, Robert Conrad, have all called for an investigation of one aspect of this matter or another by someone outside the Justice Department.

The reasons in my view are clear. When investigating allegations against the President and Vice President, the Attorney General is inherently conflicted, and any decision she may render in these matters will not inspire the public's confidence. This is particularly true of any decision not to prosecute.

While I am sure we will hear much commentary today about the provisions of the now-expired independent counsel law, the Ethics in Government Act, the provisions of which the Attorney General in my opinion incorrectly argued, unduly restricted her decision-making process. Those provisions no longer exist.

The appointment of an outside special counsel is now governed solely by Justice Department regulations, not a statute. The Attorney General possesses the authority to appoint an outside prosecutor under her own regulations when, as here, it is in the public interest.

There are many legitimate questions concerning the process at the Department that resulted in the Attorney General's refusal to appoint an independent counsel for campaign finance and the merits of those decisions. The committee will pursue those during today's hearing. There is also, however, the ongoing question of whether the Attorney General will use her authority to appoint an outside counsel under Justice Department regulations. The Attorney General certainly has the ability to do so.

I respect the Attorney General's desire to make these decisions free from outside pressure, from members of Congress, the media, and others. That is understandable. I also agree with her public comments that such a decision should be the result of a thorough and objective evaluation of the facts and the law. It seems to me, however, that the "pressure" to appoint an outside counsel is coming from inside the Justice Department, from people she has chosen at various times to advise her and to head the Campaign Finance Task Force. The Attorney General and the Justice Department have been examining these facts for 4 years now which would appear to be ample time to be thorough, and it is now time to make a decision and to be held accountable for it.

With that, we will turn to Senator Leahy.

STATEMENT OF HON. PATRICK LEAHY, A U.S. SENATOR FROM THE STATE OF VERMONT

Senator LEAHY. Thank you, Mr. Chairman.

Attorney General Reno, thank you for your cooperation and your agreement to be here today. As you probably know, this hearing will take on the air more of an inquisition than an oversight hearing, but I think you can handle that.

Before the inquisition begins, I want to commend you for making a real difference in America. Especially, since this may be the last time that you will be appearing before this committee in the role as Attorney General. You have helped stop the steady increase in the crime rate. You have worked aggressively with Federal, State, and local enforcement officers to keep violence and property crime rates down.

Under your leadership and the programs established by the Violent Crime Control and Law Enforcement Act of 1994, the Nation's serious crime rate has declined for 8 straight years. Murder rates have fallen to their lowest level in three decades. Since 1994, violent crimes by juveniles and the juvenile arrest rate for serious crimes have also declined. According to the FBI's latest crime statistics, there has been a 7-percent decline in reported serious violence and property crime from 1998 totals. All of these, certainly in my adult life, I have never seen the crime rates come down as much as they have during the time you have been Attorney General, but you have not stopped on that. You have worked to keep our schools and streets safe, and I wish the Congress would cooperate with you more.

In my longer statement, which I will put in the record, we find such things that we have not done, like the Juvenile Justice Conference stalled, frankly, by the gun lobby; hate crimes, Bulletproof Vest Partnership Act, Innocence Protection Act, domestic violence, and Justice Department nominations.

Let's talk about the independent counsel appointments, your determination not to call for the appointment of an independent counsel in connection with campaign finance, but your determination to pursue those matters through a Justice Department task force. That is a task force that you can look to as one that has had a great deal of success. It has obtained more than 20 convictions and pleas, actually a lot better than what we saw with the Special Counsel, and I am thinking of Kenneth Starr who spent over $50 million—$55.0 million—had dozens, even hundreds of FBI agents available to him over the period of time that he existed.

The bottom line on your independent counsel decisions in 1998 and 1999, where you determined rather than using the Justice Department, but rather to use independent counsel, is that after 82 days of hearings—82 days of hearings—and investigation after investigation after investigation before a series of Senate and House committees, and all the critics and all those out to undermine your authority, no one has been able to question your integrity and your independence and your decisionmaking. Not FBI Director Freeh, not Charles La Bella, nor really anybody on this committee has said they believe you sacrificed your integrity and your independent judgment to some corrupt influence.

I should also note that nobody, including the chairman of the Specter investigations, Senator Specter, has said that the Vice President has done anything wrong.

Now, I know you are going to be asked about decisions to appoint and not to appoint independent counsel. One focus I have been told will be on informal comments poorly made in 1996 by Mr. Radek, the chief of the Public Integrity Section, to FBI officials relating to whether he felt pressure because the Attorney General had not yet been reappointed to a second term.

Mr. Radek, who met frequently with these officials, does not remember any such conversation on this topic, acknowledges that he may have felt pressure to do a good job. Mr. Radek has denied the claims of the FBI that the pressure he felt was in any way related to the Attorney General's job status.

I understand that one focus of this hearing will be to explore this dispute further, and I simply do not understand how any of this, if it happened at all, bears on the Attorney General's independent counsel decision.

Those of us who appeared before this committee have repeatedly attested to the integrity of Attorney General Janet Reno. Those who talked to us, who testified before us, have repeatedly assured all of us that all decisions made by her were on the basis of her honest assessment.

Let me just tell you a couple of the things. Charles La Bella, just this last May, told the Judiciary Subcommittee on Administrative Oversight in the Courts, as part of this investigation, that his perception was that the Attorney General made no decisions to protect anyone. FBI Director Louis Freeh told the House Government Reform Committee, "I do not believe for one moment that any of her decisions, but particularly her decisions in this matter, have been motivated by anything other than the facts and the law, which she is obligated to follow." Robert Litt, just last week, said, "The Department's deliberations in this matter have now been made public. The thousands of pages of memoranda analyzing this issue, which have been released to the public, make it abundantly clear that all of the Attorney General's decisions were made solely on the merits after full and, indeed, exhaustive consideration that the facts show and legal issues involved and without any political influence at all." Larry Parkinson responded that he did not have any doubt about Attorney General Reno's integrity. This goes on and on and on.

I have been concerned about some of the oversight here. I did when the committee precipitously sent staff to Texas, barring Senator Danforth to complain that we are interfering with his investigation. I have been concerned about sending subpoenas to line attorneys who now have to be asked questions over and over again whether they are simply raising the points in a hearing or in a decision, whether they are devil's-advocating something, and will they ever do that again.

I think this is wrong. I think we are seeing now what is happening when we have cases underway; for example, Wen Ho Lee, where the committee has now received a formal request from Mr. Lee's defense attorney for the Republican report in this matter and what has been generated by it.

We have heard that sitting Federal judges on pending criminal matters had been questioned about what they are going to do by members of this committee.

I am hoping that we are not going to make the same mistake we saw when we had Kenneth Starr and a runaway operation in the House of Representatives that did not show very well on the whole Congress.

Mr. Chairman, I will put my whole statement in the record, but based on your decision to turn this from the full committee to the subcommittee, to the Specter investigation subcommittee, I will also then yield my place to the Senator from New Jersey, Mr. Torricelli.

[The prepared statement of Senator Leahy follows:]

PREPARED STATEMENT OF SENATOR PATRICK J. LEAHY

Attorney General Reno, thank you for your cooperation and your agreement to be here today. This session will more resemble an inquisition than an oversight hearing, but I expect that you are steeled for that eventuality. Before our Republican members begin the inquisition, I wanted to commend you for making a real difference in America, especially because this may be the last time you appear before this committee in your role as Attorney General. You have not only helped stop the steady increases in the crime rate but have worked aggressively with our Federal, State and local law enforcement officers to keep the violent and property crime rates in this country going down.

Under your leadership, and the programs established by the Violent Crime Control and Law enforcement Act of 1994, the nation's serious crime rate has declined for eight straight years. Murder rates have fallen to their lowest levels in three decades. Since 1994, violent crimes by juveniles and the juvenile arrest rates for serious crimes have also declined. According to the FBI's latest crime statistics, released on May 7, 2000, in just the last year, there has been a seven percent decline in reported serious violent and property crime from 1998 totals. Both murder and robbery registered eight percent drops, while forcible rape and aggravated assault figures each declined by seven percent from 1998. All Americans owe you an enormous thanks for a job well done.

Yet you have not simply rested on your laurels. I, for one, appreciate your tireless efforts to press for additional change to keep our schools and streets safe. This Congress has left much unfinished business that deserves and requires our attention.

Juvenile Justice Conference.—Last year when you joined us for the oversight hearing of the Department we were all grieving for victims of school violence in Columbine. With your help, the Senate moved swiftly to pass the Hatch-Leahy juvenile crime bill with a strong bipartisan 73-vote majority, a bill that included a number of common sense measures on gun safety and school safety. Unfortunately, despite our best efforts, your efforts and those of the President, the Republican majority will not convene the conference on that legislation to send a final bill to the President that can make a difference in the lives of Americans. If the roles were reversed and you were holding an oversight hearing on our performance, you certainly would have much to criticize.

Hate Crimes.—Last year, you joined us just as the Committee was postponing hearings on hate crimes. Unfortunately, this Committee never considered that legislation. Still, last Tuesday a strong bipartisan majority of the Senate, indeed a 57-vote majority that included a bipartisan majority from the members of this Committee, adopted the Kennedy-Smith amendment incorporating the Local Law Enforcement Enhancement Act of 2000 into legislation before the Senate. Senate adoption of this hate crimes legislation is a significant step forward. We thank you for your support of that important effort.

Bulletproof Vest Partnership Grant Act.—I hope the Republican zeal for investigating, instead of legislating, does not further delay the Committee's consideration of the bipartisan Bulletproof Vest Partnership Grant Act of 2000, which would reauthorize and double the funding for this highly successful Department of Justice grant program to provide our nation's law enforcement officers with life-saving body armor. The Department of Justice has already provided more than 90,000 bulletproof vests to law enforcement officers across the country under the 1998 law sponsored by Senator Campbell and me. I appreciate the Attorney General's support for the original Campbell-Leahy law and our reauthorization legislation.

Innocence Protection Act.—I thank you for your recent comments on the importance of ensuring competent counsel for those charged in cases that can lead to the imposition of the death penalty. I agree. That is why perhaps the most important provisions of he Leahy-Smith-LaHood-Delahunt Innocence Protection Act are those seeking to assist the States in establishing standards for competent counsel and helping provide the resources needed to ensure a fair trial.

Domestic Violence.—I also commend you for helping to stem the tide of domestic violence and for moving aggressively to help the victims of this abuse and to improve rights and services for crime victims in general. We are hopeful this week that the Committee, at long last, will report the reauthorization of the Violence Against Women Act. I would also like to see us report additional crime victims legislation without delay.

Justice Department Nominations.—I regret that the majority of this Committee and the Senate have stalled the many nominations for senior positions at the Justice Department, within law enforcement, and for the federal courts. That Dan Marcus, Randy Moss, David Ogden, and Bill Lann Lee have not been confirmed as the Associate Attorney General, Assistant Attorney General for the Office of Legal

Counsel, Assistant Attorney General for the Civil Division and Assistant Attorney General for the Civil Rights division is regrettable and inexcusable.

Independent Counsel Appointments.—I wanted to make a few pertinent observations, about your determinations not to call for the appointment of an independent counsel in connection with campaign finance but to pursue those matters through a Justice Department Task Force that has obtained more than 20 convictions and pleas—more in fact than were obtained by Kenneth Starr with all the FBI agents and more than $50 million at his disposal over a period of 5 years.

The bottom line on your independent counsel decisions in 1998 and 1999 is that after 82 days of hearings, and investigation after investigation before a series of Senate and House Committees and with leaks and critics and all those out to undermine your authority, no one has been able to question your integrity and your independence in your decision-making. Not FBI Director Freeh not Charles La Bella, not even Senator Specter has said that he believes that you sacrificed your integrity and your independent judgment to some corrupt influence. for that matter I should also note that Senator Specter has not said that the Vice President has done anything wrong.

I understand that the Attorney General today will be asked about her decision to appoint and not to appoint independent counsels. One focus, I have been told, will be on informal comments purportedly made in 1996 by Mr. Radek, the Chief of the Public Integrity Section, to FBI officials relating to whether he felt "pressure" because the Attorney General had not yet been reappointed to a second term. Mr. Radek, who met frequently with these officials, does not remember any conversation on this topic and acknowledges that he may have mentioned feeling pressure to do a good job. Mr. Radek has denied the claims of the FBI that the pressure he felt was in any way related to the Attorney General's job status. I understand that one focus of this hearing will be to explore this dispute further and I simply do not understand how any of this, if it happened at all, bears on this Attorney General's independent counsel decisions.

All of those who have appeared before this Committee have repeatedly attested to the integrity of Attorney General Janet Reno and have repeatedly assured all of us that all decisions made by her were on the basis of her honest assessment of the facts and not the result of politics. Everyone, including those people who disagreed with her on some of the independent counsel decisions, has told us this. Let me remind everyone of what we have heard:

Charles La Bella: In his May 3, 1998, press release, Mr. La Bella said that "At the end of the process, I was completely comfortable with [the Attorney General's] decision not to seek an independent counsel and with the process by which she reached that decision."

In August 1998, he told the House Government Reform Committee that the integrity and the independence of the Attorney General were "beyond reproach."

Just this May, Mr. La Bella told the Judiciary Subcommittee on Administrative Oversight and the Courts as part of this investigation that his perception was that the Attorney General "made no decisions to protect anyone."

FBI Director Louis Freeh: In August 1998, Director Freeh told the House Government Reform Committee: "I do not believe for one moment that any of her decisions, but particularly her decisions in this matter, have been motivated by anything other than the facts and the law which she is obligated to follow."

Robert Litt: Just last week, in his statement to the Subcommittee, Robert Litt said: "The Department's deliberations in this matter have now been made public. The thousands of pages of memoranda analyzing this issue which have been released to the public make it abundantly clear that all of the Attorney General's decisions were made solely on the merits, after full—indeed exhaustive—consideration of the factual and legal issues involved and without any political influences at all.

Larry Parkinson: In response to whether he had any doubt about Attorney General Reno's integrity, FBI General Counsel Larry Parkinson responded: "No I do not," at the May 24, 2000 Subcommittee hearing on this issue.

The endless oversight on the topic of independent counsels has confirmed over and over again that the process worked. Some may disagree with some of the ultimate decisions, but that should not be the focus of oversight. Rather, the object of oversight should be to make sure that the process worked; that decisions were made on the basis of facts; and that judgments were not influenced by politics. We know that the process worked and that the Attorney General's decisions were made in good faith, relying on good prosecutorial judgment and after full consideration of all the facts as well as of the conflicting opinions of many different advisors.

In the guise of "oversight," this Committee has inappropriately politicized ongoing investigations. There should be no mistake about it: I believe that oversight by the Committee can be of great importance. That oversight must be conducted in a careful and considered manner. I have expressed my concerns about this hydra-headed investigation on a number of occasions. I noted my concern when some on the Committee precipitously sent staff to Texas, prompting Special Counsel Danforth to complain about this Committee's interference with his investigation into what happened at the Branch Davidian compound in Waco.

I do not believe that line attorneys and line agents should be called to testify in oversight matters unless there are some sort of exceptional circumstances—like internal corruption. I worry about the long-term effects that some of the actions taken in these investigations may have. This Senate Judiciary Committee now issues subpoenas on a regular basis to hard-working and dedicated government employees. This Committee has subpoenaed past and present line attorneys to talk about long-ago disagreements with supervisors—even though everyone recognizes that line attorneys are not the ultimate decision-makers. Members of the Committee have launched personalized attacks on the credentials, integrity, capability and credibility of experienced and dedicated prosecutors. I am extremely concerned that these tactics have harmed individuals, the Justice Department as an institution, and as a result the American people.

The Committee has already heard from Wen Ho Lee's defense lawyers and we are now being drawn into that ongoing prosecution. I will not be surprised if other defense counsel, who have been monitoring Senator Specter's hearings, use those hearings as a basis for defense motions to undercut other prosecutions by the Campaign Finance Task Force of the Department of Justice. These are other risks of delving prematurely into ongoing criminal matters.

I had been warning over the last several months that this Committee was crossing lines that it should not cross when it made subpoenaing of line attorneys and agents its practice and began interfering in ongoing criminal investigations. Last week and this represent the culmination of those errors as we now have a circumstance in which leaks and innuendo about an ongoing matter have led you to being called before this Committee to be quizzed incessantly over open investigative matters that you cannot appropriately discuss.

I know that you will resist political pressure from any source, even this Committee, when it comes to your exercise of your prosecutorial judgment. You and I both recall that this Republican Senate has been trying to pressure you to appoint a special counsel since 1997. This Republican Senate has been telling you how to do your job and exercise your judgment, although it has not done a very good job of fulfilling its own legislative responsibilities to the American people. Sometimes I have wondered out loud whether it is because of their lack of an effective legislative agenda that this Republican Senate has chosen to investigate rather than legislate.

I had thought that I had seen it all. That is, until last week, when a Member of this Committee held a press conference to discuss rumors about confidential matters that may or may not actually be occurring at the Department of Justice. This Member stated on national television that his information did not come by way of "leaks" and that it had properly been disclosed to him in the course of the "official" oversight investigation. My request for a bipartisan briefing on this new supposedly "official" and non-leaked information has been summarily brushed aside. That is not how we operated when he conducted a successful bipartisan investigation into the events at Ruby Ridge. The partisan and political nature of these proceedings could not be more transparent.

The American public should know of the political influence this Republican investigation is attempting to assert on PENDING matters at the Justice Department because it is shocking.

Consider some of the things that have already occurred:
—a Republican Member of this Committee questioned a sitting federal judge about a case (the Peter Lee case) in which the defendant has a motion to terminate his probation—the interrogation by this Republican Member could well be viewed as an improper attempt to influence the judge's upcoming decision on this motion;
—Republican Members of this Committee have publicly urged prosecutors to take certain positions at the upcoming sentencing of a defendant Maria Hsia in one of the pending campaign finance cases. United States Senators should not be pressuring prosecutors to take certain positions—we rely on prosecutors to exercise their considerable judgment in these matters. Of course, in this instance, since attorneys to both parties to that case—the Justice Department and Ms. Hsia—were present at that hearing, I am confident that each will take whatever steps necessary to protect the rights of both parties;
—Republican Members insisted on conducting "oversight" of the Wen Ho Lee matter even though they well knew an investigation was pending. Sure enough, this Committee has now received formal requests from Mr. Lee's defense attorney for the

Republican report on the matter and for other documents generated during the course of this oversight. And this is just the beginning. It would not surprise me if we received more requests for information from Lee's attorney as that case proceeds;

—Republican staffers were sent to Waco to interview witnesses even before Senator Dunforth had an opportunity to do so. This resulted in angry letters from Senator Danforth warning this Committee not to interfere in his investigation.

We have seen it over and over again—attempts to influence pending matters because of politics. Republicans insinuate that the Attorney General's decisions on campaign finance matters were somehow influenced by politics—yet everyone, even those who disagreed, have repeatedly and forcefully attested to her independence, her integrity and her dedication to relying on the facts and the law and nothing else. It is Republican Senators, not Attorney General Reno, who are trying to make this political and insist on behaving as partisans. It was not too long ago that Kenneth Starr and the House Republicans foisted a partisan, expensive and debilitating impeachment on the Senate and the country. The repeated misuse of the investigative and hearing apparatus of congressional committees for political campaigning by other means is a troubling legacy of the Republican-led Congress that history will not forgive. It is all the more troubling when the political investigative and hearing machinery are injected into our justice system. It seems that some are intent on retreading that road for partisan political gain and have already forgotten the lessons of the last several years.

The CHAIRMAN. We will now take the statements of the chairman of the subcommittee and the ranking member, Senator Specter and then Senator Torricelli, and then we will listen to the Attorney General.

STATEMENT OF HON. ARLEN SPECTER, A U.S. SENATOR FROM THE STATE OF PENNSYLVANIA

Senator SPECTER. Thank you, Mr. Chairman.

At the outset, let me observe that the Spanish Inquisition would really marvel at this proceeding today under these Klieg lights, out in the public, and a comment or two about Wen Ho Lee, where the subcommittee has recommended specific legislation which has been supported by the full committee, and to correct the misstatement about judges on pending matters, Judge Hatter was questioned about a closed matter, and the only judge at issue, but on to the subject matter at hand, I join in welcoming you here, Attorney General Reno.

The focus of what the subcommittee has been doing involves espionage cases, campaign finance, and Waco. With respect to the issue of independent counsel, a good bit of our focus today will be about your decisions not to appoint independent counsel, and by way of setting the stage, with respect to your judgment not to have independent counsel as to the Vice President.

As to the distinction between hard money and soft money and whether the Vice President knew that he was soliciting hard money, the established record shows that four witnesses testified that hard money was discussed in the Vice President's presence at the famous November 21st meeting; that one of the witnesses, Leon Panetta even went so far as to point out that, "The purpose of the meeting was to make sure they knew what the hell was going on"; that included among those four witnesses was the Vice President's Chief of Staff David Strauss who had a written memorandum putting in writing the fact that there was a discussion about 35-percent hard money. Then there were the 13 memoranda from Harold Ickes which went to the Vice President marked "hard money" and the testimony of the Vice President's assistant that they very carefully culled the in-box to leave out matters that the Vice President wanted excluded, but always left in the items with respect to what Mr. Ickes had sent, and then the Vice President's own statement that, the subject matter of the memorandums would have already been discussed in his and the President's presence. The Vice President further acknowledged that he, had been a candidate for 16 years and had a good understanding of the hard money.

At this point, it is important to put in perspective that the independent counsel law then in effect did not call for a conclusion that the Vice President had committed the crime, but only that there was specific and credible information, not evidence, just information, that there may—and I emphasize the word "may"—have been a violation of the Federal criminal laws.

Then there is the question of the coffees, 103 of them, some $26 million contributed, over $7 million within one month of the donors' attendance. The Vice President was questioned about this matter on April 18. Question: "In terms of a fundraising tool, what was the purpose of the coffee?" Answer: "I don't know." Further down, page 53: "With respect to raising the $108 million, did you have discussions with anybody concerning the roles that coffee would play in raising that type of money?" Answer: "Well, let me define the term 'raising' if I could." Shades of what "is" is. At page 59, question: "You had indicated earlier that you may have attended one coffee. What were you talking about?" Answer, a little farther down, page 60: "Although it was not my practice to go to any of these coffees, there may have been one—one that I attended briefly perhaps because some of the invitees were known to me."

Then the attorney for the Vice President submitted a letter on the subject, 2 days later, pointing out that according to the Vice President's schedule, he was designated to attend four White House coffees and the Vice President hosted approximately 21 coffees in the Executive Office Building.

Very briefly on the issue of the Buddhist Temple, to put the matter in perspective, shortly before the scheduled fundraiser, the Vice President's scheduler sent him an e-mail message asking whether he would be interested in adding another stop on the April 29 itinerary on top of the "two fundraisers in San Jose and L.A." The Vice President responded: If we already have booked the fundraisers, then we have to decline.

Again, Ickes' memos were specific to the President about a $250,000 take from a fundraiser, and a second one, a $325,000 take from a fundraiser. It is in this context, Madam Attorney General Reno, that we raise the question about the lower level of sufficiency to establish with specific and credible information the level for calling for independent counsel.

Again, as I said last Thursday, in fairness to the Vice President, it is a very different level of evidence than that required for a criminal prosecution or for an indictment.

One of the issues in sharp focus today will be why on the first four times the Vice President was questioned, he was never asked about the Hsi Lai Buddhist Temple. It was only when the subcommittee issued subpoenas and had the La Bella and Freeh memoranda with a return date of April 20 that the Department of

Justice finally got around to questioning the Vice President on April 18.

So this is a brief focus, in addition to the decision that you made not to appoint independent counsel, with President Clinton and the Vice President on the soft money coordination issue, and advice of counsel.

One final comment. The Vice President's surrogates have raised an issue that my disclosure of what Mr. Conrad recommended was inappropriate. That disclosure was made in the course of the Committee's business, but before making that disclosure, we called in Robert Conrad and asked him the questions head on, and it was only when he failed to disclose them did the disclosure come from the subcommittee. That was done so that there could be public accountability.

There was a substantial period of time between the La Bella recommendation and the Freeh recommendation, the Freeh recommendation in November of 1997 and the La Bella recommendation in July 1998, until we finally got the specifics on their memoranda on April 20 in the year 2000. I do not take lightly the comments of the Vice President's surrogates accusing me of McCarthy-like tactics and being in cahoots with the Bush campaign. I have not, and would not, discuss this matter with the Bush campaign. As to the reference of McCarthy-like tactics, that is a matter which I will take up personally with the Vice President to see if it was authorized, and if so, I will take it up with him in some substantial detail.

Thank you, Mr. Chairman.

The CHAIRMAN. Thank you, Senator Specter.

We will turn to Senator Torricelli. Senator Thurmond has to leave. He says he has a very short statement, and we will grant him that time. Then we are going to go to the Attorney General.

STATEMENT OF HON. ROBERT G. TORRICELLI, A U.S. SENATOR FROM THE STATE OF NEW JERSEY

Senator TORRICELLI. Thank you, Mr. Chairman. Madam Attorney General, good afternoon.

Madam Attorney General, I welcome you to the committee and thank you very much for your attendance today, hoping that at long last through your testimony and questions that we are about to ask, we can bring what has been a matter that has proceeded for literally years to some conclusion.

I think, Madam Attorney General, it would be fair to say, as I begin my own statement, that not only do I hold no brief for the Attorney General, but indeed, I have on occasions not hesitated to criticize judgments of the Justice Department when I found reason to disagree with them.

Indeed, in the matter of Wen Ho Lee and the prosecution of Peter Lee, I have expressed my concerns, joined with the Republican majority in their investigations, and never hesitated to reach a judgment on how I believe the matters should have been dealt with differently, but it is inconceivable to me that either the Justice Department generally or Janet Reno specifically could be criticized on questions with regard to either her independence, which raises issue of integrity, or her willingness to use the independent counsel statute. The facts simply do not support either.

Indeed, the only area of criticism open to those who are raising issues with regard to the independent counsel statute is that on occasion they simply do not agree with the final judgment. No Attorney General could be less vulnerable to attack on issues of independence. No Attorney General could be less vulnerable to attack on issues of using the independent counsel statute or using outside counsel when otherwise generally necessary.

On several different occasions, Janet Reno has appointed independent counsels to investigate the President of the United States, for whom I assume she has both affection and loyalty, and fellow members of the Cabinet. Not simply more than any other Attorney General in the history of the United States, but more than her predecessors combined, she has sat across a Cabinet table with colleagues and friends and appointed independent counsels, I assume, at some personal discomfort because it was the right thing to do and the facts justified it.

I do not even make this claim because I necessarily agree with all those instances in which she appointed an independent counsel. Indeed, I believe she has erred on the side of appointing them even when not always justifiable. At enormous cost in human terms and to the taxpayers, we have witnessed independent counsels being named against former Agriculture Secretary Mike Espy, who was prosecuted for accepting sports tickets, but who after 4 years and a $17 million investigation was acquitted on all 30 counts.

Housing Secretary Cisneros charged with felonies related to his relationship with a woman, plead guilty to a misdemeanor after a multimillion-dollar investigation and paid a $10,000 fine.

The matter of Ken Starr, his judgment, his cost, his investigation speaks for itself.

Yet, incredibly, incredulously, the Attorney General of the United States now faces this Congress with the allegation that she has hesitated to appoint an independent counsel on another matter. Her independence, her integrity and her willingness to examine her own administration are being brought into question.

The issue now before the committee appears to be centered on whether when confronted with appointing an independent counsel under the statute previously or now under internal Justice Department guidelines there was unanimity on her judgment. Indeed, wouldn't it have been extraordinary if upon soliciting advice from all of her assistants, in Public Integrity, the Criminal Division, her deputy, each of these people had reviewed all the facts, considered the law, and reached the same judgment? If there is one thing that characterizes the difference between Janet Reno's judgment in dealing with whether to appoint an independent counsel on the campaign-related issues with the Vice President and the seven other instances involving the President and members of the Cabinet, it is the breadth of advice that she sought, not simply from all of her own senior advisors, but from the director of the FBI and the leadership of the Campaign Finance Task Force.

Some members seem to react with extraordinary surprise that there was a difference of judgment. The surprise, however, would have been if they were all of the same mind and all came to the same judgment, given the extensive number of people that were consulted, indeed the unprecedented number of people that were questioned.

Among those consulted was, perhaps one of the more senior officials of the Justice Department, Mr. Radek, a professional of no particular partisan persuasion, 29 years with the Department of Justice, 20 of those years with the Public Integrity Section. Mr. Radek appeared before our committee. He concluded, and I quote, "There was no substantive basis to proceed under the clause of the statute." He further shared with the committee not that it was his judgment nor that of a majority of his staff nor of an overwhelming majority of his staff, but that it was the unanimous judgment of career prosecutors in the Public Integrity Section that there was no basis for using the mandatory provisions of the independent counsel statute with regard to Vice President Gore. He further added to the committee that had there been an independent counsel and we proceeded under the mandatory provisions of the law, there was no evidence upon which to build a case with regard to Vice President Gore.

During the course of the Attorney General's review of a preliminary inquiry of the facts, it must be assumed by those who think that a misjudgment was made by the Attorney General in not appointing an independent counsel that she made her judgment without a complete review of the law or the facts as they apply to the Vice President. The record is directly the opposite.

250 witnesses were interviewed, including the Vice President. Thousands of documents were obtained from the White House, the DNC, the Clinton-Gore campaign, and a variety of individuals who received telephone calls from the Vice President. It was on this basis that Mr. Radek and each and every one of the career prosecutors of the Justice Department advised the Attorney General that she should not proceed and, if she proceeded, there was no case to be made.

It is worth noting that Mr. Radek is the single individual in the Department of Justice with the greatest experience in the application of the independent counsel statute, the most experienced in law enforcement, the most experienced with the statute, and the most experienced with campaign finance-related issues. Indeed, his combined staff has a multitude of years of experience compared to Mr. La Bella, Mr. Conrad, and Mr. Freeh on campaign-related issues and issues relating to the statute.

Indeed, Mr. Radek testified before our committee that he believed that it was significant that his own staff had more experience specifically with the statute, and that the other individuals involved had little and in some cases none.

Now the statute has expired. In its place the Attorney General has enacted regulations providing for an office of special counsel to handle those cases that once would have been referred to an independent counsel. It is worth noting that the Attorney General was not required to write these procedures, to establish special counsel provision within Justice, but she did so. It was the right thing to do, and now she has followed those procedures.

The question then turns to the individual instances that are leading some to question the Attorney General's judgment with regard to independent counsels. Before briefly examining the three instances, I want simply to point out to my colleagues, that this is not the first time that I have been in this hearing room on these issues addressing these questions. As indeed three successive Campaign Finance Task Force heads have led inquiries, so too the Government Affairs Committee occupied months and thousands of hours of review of some of these same issues.

Indeed, over the course of 3 years, the House and Senate expended $11 million, questioned hundreds of people, only to have their own efforts duplicated by the Justice Department and the FBI itself, the same issues, the same law, the same facts, only to be assumed to the same equation. It was not for lack of effort or desire or motivation that Mr. Thompson and the bipartisan members of this committee could find no substantive basis to find violations of the law by the President of the Vice President. We came to the same conclusion as Mr. Radek and professional prosecutors within the Justice Department.

Let me turn to each of these three instances. First, the visit to the Buddhist Temple. It is alleged that the Vice President knew that he was attending a fundraiser at a charitable non-profit institution, the Buddhist Temple, where violations of the law occurred. The Government Affairs Committee examined this issue. No doubt, the Justice Department has done so again.

We found the following. No tickets were sold. No campaign materials were displayed. No campaign table was set up for information, solicitation, or acceptance of money. The Vice President made no mention of fundraising in his speech, but spoke about religious tolerance and brotherhood.

The committee was further persuaded that the only paper the Vice President actually received on that day in visiting the Buddhist Temple was his schedule. His schedule makes no mention of a fundraiser, solicitation of funds, people raising funds, commitment to the campaign or involvement in the campaign. The only paper before the Vice President of the United States was instructions that he was to extend brief remarks from the podium and exit, take photos with 150 guests, pay homage in the shrine. This is a fundraiser? This is leading the Vice President of the United States to solicit funds? $11 million later, Mr. Chairman, this is what our committee found.

With respect to the White House coffees, according to the popular press it appears that the Campaign Finance Task Force was intrigued by the number of coffees that were held. The Vice President in answering their questions relied upon the belief that the question was as to coffees held in the White House. The Vice President seemed to have answered that question both honestly and accurately. Upon reflection, there are some who are now arguing that the question did not differentiate between coffees held in the Old Executive Office Building, of which there were a greater number, and those held at the White House. This is the nature of a Federal law enforcement inquiry? This question of whether or not we were distinguishing between the appropriate buildings of the White House complex and the numbers of coffees is the basis of a serious allegation of perjury? On what basis could it be argued that the Vice President was attempting to mislead someone.

The Justice Department knew how many coffees were held. The popular press, the American people, and the Justice Department knew where they were held, the numbers that were held, and who was in attendance. The facts were not material, they were not new, and they misled no one, nor did the Vice President clearly have the intention to do so.

The third issue at hand is the solicitation of hard, as opposed to soft, money. The allegation centers largely on a single meeting in which 15 people were in attendance. They have all been interviewed by committees of the Congress, by the Justice Department, and by the task force. There has been a great deal of attention paid to the fact that two people—two—remember a mention of hard money. At a later date after reviewing documentation, a third raised the possibility. There were 15 people there.

Apparently, if the President and the Vice President of the United States do not remember a discussion of hard money, they have good company because neither did 12 other people. The entire charge rests on the belief that the Vice President of the United States reads every memorandum that reaches his desk, every word that is ever said at a meeting, and nothing is ever to be forgotten. That somehow these two individuals have extraordinary credibility in their recall, but another 12 do not, including the President and the Vice President, and this is alleged to be an offense which would warrant the appointment of an independent counsel.

Madam Attorney General, the best conclusion to be reached on how you have performed your responsibilities as Attorney General, the integrity with which you have come to your position, the independence with which you have weighed your judgment, is that somehow through all these years, you have managed to have everybody disagree with you on something, at some time, in some way. Good for you. That is the way Attorneys General should be.

I am among those who have disagreed with you, but I cannot argue that you did not err on the side of independence, that you did not have the courage to look the President of the United States in the eye, and Cabinet member who I know you have great affection for, and have served with over the years, and questioned them when they were wrong and stood up for what needed to be done.

It is, Mr. Chairman, though we will endure this hearing today, time to bring these long proceedings to a close.

A New York Times editorial on Sunday may have actually put it in the best perspective. These issues now belong to the American people. Vice President Gore may have made some mistakes of judgment. I do not believe he made mistakes of law. I commend those questions now to the American voter. Vice President Gore, like all Americans, deserves to be judged by the totality of his record and his service. He has done some things he would like to change. He has done a great deal that is good.

I hope, Mr. Chairman, after several years of reviewing the same questions and the same facts, which always seem to come to the same conclusion, this can finally come to an end. And I hope that somehow, despite all the doubts and the cynicism, we can have some confidence in professionals at the Justice Department who have reviewed this for so many years and seem to overwhelmingly agree with the Attorney General. Even those who disagreed with the Attorney Genearl on the facts and would have decided differently have said they respect those in the Department who saw it differently and do not question the Attorney General's independence or integrity. They believe that justice was done. If Mr. Freeh, Mr. La Bella, and Mr. Conrad can come to that judgment, so can we.

Thank you, Mr. Chairman.

The CHAIRMAN. Thank you, Senator.

Senator Thurmond has asked for just a short statement, and then we are going to turn to the Attorney General.

STATEMENT OF HON. STROM THURMOND, A U.S. SENATOR FROM THE STATE OF SOUTH CAROLINA

Senator THURMOND. I have an urgent appointment, and I thank Senator Hatch for his kindness.

Mr. Chairman, our Nation is built upon a system of laws that the Attorney General is duty bound to uphold. The issue of appointing an independent counsel to investigate the 1996 Clinton-Gore campaign fundraising irregularities has tested our duty like nothing else, and thus far, Ms. Reno has failed to meet her obligations in this matter.

This committee has been calling on the Attorney General to appoint an outside counsel for over 3 years. We are not alone. The Director of the FBI, a former judge, has repeatedly told her that she has no other choice, and her hand-picked career prosecutor, Mr. Charles La Bella, agreed. Even a top Justice Department official who has always been a strong defender of the administration, Mr. Robert Litt, recommended an independent counsel for the Vice President. It seems that about the only top advisor to the Attorney General who always felt otherwise was Mr. Lee Radek, who even admitted to the FBI back in 1996 that his office was under pressure about recommending an independent counsel because the Attorney General's job might hang in the balance.

We learned last week that the current chief of the campaign finance investigation, Mr. Robert Conrad, who is also a career prosecutor, apparently has concluded that a special counsel is needed. The Attorney General was reportedly angry about the disclosure of Mr. Conrad's recommendation and has opened an investigation. However she has no one to blame but herself. If she had appointed an independent counsel when she had a duty to do so under the statute, this matter would have been over a long time ago, and the Vice President may have been exonerated. In any event, as it stands, a dark cloud hangs over the Vice President. Yet, again, we have serious issues raised about the truthfulness of our top elected officials in the current administration when they are questioned under oath.

The cloud will remain until this matter is properly and fully investigated by someone outside the Department of Justice. By avoiding the inevitable, it is the Attorney General, not unnamed sources in the Justice Department or this committee, who are doing a disservice to the Vice President. We must always work to maintain the people's confidence in the fairness and the impartiality of our system of justice.

Today, the public has no confidence in the way the campaign finance investigation has been handled. The only way to remedy this and to restore public trust is to appoint a special counsel.

So I encourage the Attorney General yet again to appoint a special counsel, but I have no confidence that she will. If she would not do so when the plain words of the independent counsel law required it, it is wishful thinking to expect that she will exercise her discretion to appoint one now. But we must continue to encourage her to do what is right once and for all.

Thank you, Mr. Chairman.

The CHAIRMAN. Thank you, Senator Thurmond.

Madam Attorney General, welcome to the committee. We turn the time over to you.

STATEMENT OF HON. JANET RENO, ATTORNEY GENERAL, U.S. DEPARTMENT OF JUSTICE, WASHINGTON, DC

Attorney General RENO. Good afternoon, Mr. Chairman and members of the committee.

Since my first hearing before you on March 9th, 1993, we have worked together in a bipartisan matters on many issues that affect the American people in very significant ways. I am very proud and very grateful for the opportunity to work with you, and I want to thank you all for the thoughtfulness and the kindness that you have shown me.

Mr. Chairman, I understand that you sometimes think I am crazy when I tell you that I appreciate the oversight function, but I have before this committee because it brings new issues to our attention, and it sharpens our decision-making at the Department of Justice. I moan and groan as I get ready for them, but I always find them helpful.

In the course of these oversight functions and committees, we have debated and disagreed, sometimes fiercely, on a number of issues, and today, obviously, is no exception, but I think our Founding Fathers valued the spirit of spirited debate and thought it one of the most important foundations of our Government.

I am going to take just a moment to reflect on something. One of the most extraordinary experiences that I have had as Attorney General is to welcome my colleagues, Ministers of Justice, Ministers of the Interior, law enforcement officials from the emerging democracies to my conference room, to look at how they act almost with stars in their eyes as they are commenced on a great new undertaking. To see some of them fail and some of the succeed makes you realize how fragile democracy is and what a cherished institution it is and how we must not take it for granted.

This scene is the epitome of democracy. It represents the hallmarks of it, representative government, public accountability, and the peaceful transfer of power. It is almost a miracle, but it is a great testament to the strength and the wonder of the human spirit.

It is a miracle that we have a Constitution that had stood the test of time in the advance of technology that our Founding Fathers never dreamed would be possible, but at the heart of that document, essentially and required is the respect for individuals and the different opinions we hold. Although I may disagree with so many of you on so many occasions and agree with you completely on others, I respect you and I respect your opinion.

In this spirit, the Department has tried very hard to cooperate with and facilitate the oversight process, thus following the long-standing executive branch policy and practice of seeking to accommodate congressional requests for information to the fullest extent with the constitutional and statutory obligations of the executive branch.

A Constitution also wisely assigns each branch of Government distinct and limited roles. Among the most important functions of the Justice Department as part of the executive branch is the faithful execution of the laws, including the vigorous but fair prosecution of criminals.

When there is conflict between the legislative and executive branch, I want to—and I think our task as public servants is to find solutions that respects our individual duties and permits both branches to do their job responsibly.

One issue will come out today, amongst many others, that I think I have got to address because I think it will require no comment on a number of occasions, and that is I do not think it proper for me to comment on pending investigations and pending prosecutions. I think those matters should be handled thoughtfully and professionally, not in headlines, but in courtrooms and in the processes of an investigation. I mean no disrespect whatsoever to the committee when I tell you that I cannot comment. I just feel very strongly that we must be careful in order to protect the investigation, protect leads, protect the reputation of people involved, lest information disseminated impede our careful and professional process that we pursue.

I know that some of you have been concerned about the Department response, and if we have not done it as well as you would like, I will keep trying harder in the time I have remaining. There is always opportunity for improvement, but at the same time, people should be careful to reflect accurately on a situation.

First, we are required by law to review material for privacy, grand jury secrecy, and other obligations. That takes time.

Second, we have competing demands from many Senators and Members of the House who each express a very strong sense of urgency about his or her own request, all at the same time.

Third, the offices at the Department are poised to respond to these requests, but they operate under statutory caps on personnel and salaries, despite marked increases in requests on these offices by the various committees of Congress. In addition, the same people who are responding to the document requests and requests for information are also the people that are trying to move what you and I would consider to be the agenda of the American people alone.

Fourth, and most importantly, the Department has in my view been very responsive. It has produced to this committee alone more than 8,000 pages in May and June relating to the appointment of independent counsels. We have produced or given access to tens of thousands of documents on Peter Lee, Wen Ho Lee, Johnny Chung, John Huang, Charlie Trie, and Maria Hsia, among others, over 800 pages on the Loral waiver issue and over a half-a-million pages on Waco.

Last, and importantly, we must be careful not to confuse our inability to provide you with certain material as being unresponsive. If I determine that a particular document's dissemination will interfere with an ongoing investigation of criminal prosecution and cannot provide that document to you at a particular time, this is not in my view being unresponsive. I am required by law to provide answers to you that you may not like, but I can assure each of you that much thought and reflection goes into a decision to say that I can't do this. This is not a matter I or anyone at the Department takes lightly, and it in no way indicates disrespect for the committee.

Much comment has been made about how I do things and who I rely on. I urge you to read carefully the filings made with the court on the matters relating to the independent counsel, for these are the documents where I have laid out the thorough investigation of the facts at issue, the careful analysis of the law involved, and the consistent reasoned application of the law to the facts that has gone into each of these matters.

This work is complex. It is fact-intensive. Sound bites and quick appraisals are not conducive to thorough analysis. People's reputation often rests on how we talk about important matters. I urge you to read carefully the documents submitted. I think that these documents may provide additional information that would be helpful.

I value honest debate about all matters that come before me. I don't like "yes people." Somebody said some of my decisions are unanimous. I don't think I have ever had a unanimous decision one way or the other. I think the mix has always been interesting. It is no secret by now that I rely on a wide variety of people, nor do I count up the votes on each side. I don't say the majority wins or I don't say this person wins. I make the best judgment I can.

Under the independent counsel statute, when it existed, Congress placed on me the responsibility to make the judgment. I made the best judgment I could, and I will continue to try to do that.

As I told you once, Mr. Chairman, I don't do things based on polls. I do things based on the evidence and the law.

Senator Specter has commented on one of the particular cases, and has said that the standard for determining the appointment of a special counsel is that there be specific and credible information that a crime may have been committed. That is the standard that has been used not for the application of independent counsel, but for the triggering of a preliminary investigation which was done in the case to which he refers, and there is a provision for a preliminary investigation which is permitted and authorized by the Act. That was triggered. The preliminary investigation was conducted, but the bottom line at that point was in determining whether the application should be made was whether reasonable--it was necessary to have further investigation, and whether further investigation was reasonable and warranted.

Thus, I think we look at each of the standards and try our best to make the best judgment we can, and I will look forward to that opportunity to talk with you today about it.

I have said when I appeared before you last that the American people should be extraordinarily proud of the people in the Department of Justice. If you want to blame somebody, if you reach disagreement, blame me. Don't blame them. They work so hard for you. They try to give you the best advice they can.

Director Freeh will disagree with me, but he has done so much for this country. There are people that you never hear about that do incredible jobs going over the law, getting the facts, agents, border patrol officers, just so many different people in so many different ways. The American people should be very proud of them, and you, since many of them have served through one administration after another, should be equally proud of them. I know that I am, and I appreciate the opportunity to be here today, Mr. Chairman.

[The prepared statement of Attorney General Reno follows:]

PREPARED STATEMENT OF JANET RENO

Good afternoon, Mr. Chairman and Members of the Committee.

Since my first hearing before the Committee on march 9, 1993, we have worked together, in a bipartisan manner, on a number of important law enforcement initiatives. I am proud and grateful for the opportunity to work with you on so many matters important to the American people. I want to thank you for the thoughtfulness and kindness you have shown me over these years.

We have debated and disagreed on a number of issues. Today, I expect, there will be disagreement about matters involving the now expired Independent Counsel statute and the Department's Campaign Financing investigation. But, the founding fathers valued spirited debate as much as anything. I have told you this before, Mr. Chairman, I appreciate Congressional oversight. It brings new issues to our attention and it sharpens our decisionmaking at the Department.

Our democracy must be cherished—we cannot take it for granted—its hallmarks are representative government, public accountability, and the peaceful transfer of power. And it is a miracle or a testament to the American spirit that we govern ourselves according to a Constitution that has stood the test of time and the advance of technology. But at the heart of that document is respect for individuals and the different opinions we often hold. Although we may disagree, I respect you and your opinions.

In this spirit, the Department tries very hard to cooperate with and facilitate the oversight process, thus following the longstanding Executive Branch policy and practice of seeking to accommodate Congressional requests for information to the fullest extent consistent with the constitutional and statutory obligations of the Executive Branch. Attorney General William French Smith captured the essence of the accommodation process in a 1981 opinion: "The accommodation required is not simply an exchange of concessions or a test of political strength. It is an obligation of each branch to make a principled effort to acknowledge, and if possible to meet, the legitimate needs of the other branch." [Opinion of the Attorney General for the President, *Assertion of Executive Privilege in Response to a Congressional Subpoena*, 5 Op. O.L.C. 27, 31 (1981).]

The Constitution wisely assigns each branch of government a distinct and limited role. Among the most important functions of the Justice Department as a part of the Executive Branch is the faithful execution of the laws which includes the vigorous but fair prosecution of criminals. When there is conflict between the Legislative and Executive Branch—our task as public servants is to find solutions that respect our individual duties and permit both branches to do our jobs responsibly.

One issue that will arise today is how we deal with open investigations. I cannot discuss most aspects of an ongoing investigation, lest information disseminated impede our careful and professional conduct of these important law enforcement matters.

Another example of that accommodation is how we respond to your requests for documents about matters we are charged with investigating and prosecuting. The Department has to date produced hundreds of thousands of pages of documents responsive to your requests, and is continuing to produce materials. We have done so despite our deep concerns about the consequences of public release of much of this material. I know your Committee has been very sensitive to many of our concerns, particularly where the personal privacy of individuals is concerned, and I am grateful for that.

During my time as Attorney General, Congressional oversight requests have implicated important Departmental institutional interests with respect to ongoing law enforcement and litigation matters, pre-decisional deliberative documents on completed matters, and testimony or interviews from line attorneys. I have been particularly concerned about the oversight requests regarding ongoing law enforcement matters. Although Congress has a legitimate interest in determining how the Department enforces statutes, Congressional inquiries during the pendency of a matter pose an inherent threat to the integrity of the Department's enforcement functions. Such inquiries inescapably create the risk that the public and the courts will perceive undue political and Congressional influence over law enforcement decisions.

I have also been concerned by the recent frequent efforts to breach our line attorney policy. The Department needs to ensure that its line attorneys can exercise the independent judgment essential to the integrity of law enforcement and litigation functions and to public confidence in those decisions. By questioning the Department's Senate-confirmed leadership and if necessary, component supervisors, Congress can fulfill its oversight responsibilities without undermining the independence of line attorneys. I ask all of you to consider the demoralizing and chilling effect of the recent line attorney questioning on the dedicated career government employees who carry the major burden of our law enforcement efforts.

I recognize that the Department's efforts to safeguard the Department's institutional interests have often led Congressional Committees to express great frustration and impatience in the course of their oversight inquiries. But our law enforcement responsibilities require that the leadership of the Department always have these interests in mind when we respond to oversight inquiries. I appreciate the Senate Judiciary Committee's willingness to work closely with us in the process whereby Committees and the Department seek a mutual accommodation of Committee oversight needs and Departmental institutional concerns. It is our experience that good faith negotiations during the accommodation process almost always result in an acceptable resolution.

Mr. Chairman, you and other members of this Committee have asked to know why I've made the decisions I have in the past with respect to Independent Counsel decisions and the Campaign Finance Task Force. I urge you to read carefully the filings made with the Court on these matters—for these are the documents where I have laid out the thorough investigation of the facts at issue, the careful analysis of the law involved and the consistent, reasoned application of the law to the facts that has gone into each of these matters.

So much of what you as Senators and I as Attorney General are called to work on is complex and fact intensive. Sound bites and quick appraisals are not conducive to thorough analysis. People's reputations often rest on how we talk about important matters. I urge you to read carefully the documents submitted in the past. I think that the complete documents explaining why we made our decisions will be most useful to you.

I want to explain to you today—as best I can—how I approach these decisions.

I value honest debate about all matters that come before me—whether they are Independent Counsel decisions or matters of less or more significance. It is no secret by now that I have no particular use for "yes people." Nor do I count up the votes on each side of an issue and go with the majority. Mine is a deliberative process in which I consider not the number of people who hold a particular viewpoint or what the polls say, but the reasons behind the recommendations brought to me.

I rely on the good work of attorneys and investigators at the Department, including the work of the task Force, past and present. These prosecutors and investigators assumed a difficult task under intense pressure and the intense glare of constant scrutiny from the media and the Congress. To date they have responsibility for more than 120 investigations, convicted 20 individuals and one corporation; and more trials are pending. Their work and the cases they have brought have illuminated the difficulties that our inadequate campaign financing laws place on those who seek to address abuses of our election system. They have my great respect, admiration and gratitude, and deserve the appreciation of the nation for a job well done.

This group of dedicated career employees serve as one good example of the 124,000 employees of the Department of Justice, hard working men and women who serve the American people here and around the world every day. They uphold our liberties. They prosecute crime—from street crimes to sophisticated white collar schemes. They catch spies, cybercriminals, drug lords and terrorists. They stand guard at our borders. All around the country, the Justice Department and its law enforcement components are full partners with police, mayors and neighborhoods in preventing crime wherever possible and in the 24–7 world of protecting the public. As a nation, we are grateful for their dedication and hard work.

In the end, I am responsible for decisions of the Department, including those concerning Independent Counsels. Congress ensured this when it drafted the Independent Counsel Act and it ensured my further and increased responsibility and accountability in this area when you allowed that statute to lapse and to let regulations put in place by the Department govern the appointment of Special Counsels by the Attorney General.

I make my decisions on the facts as I see them, the significance of the evidence as I weigh it, and the law as I interpret it. I do not come to these decisions lightly nor in a vacuum.

Much has been made of the fact that several people have advised me at various times to seek the appointment of an Independent Counsel when I ultimately decided not to do so. This should come as no surprise to anyone. In each and every instance—whether I sought the appointment of an Independent Counsel or not—there were always people of the opposite view who weighed in thoughtfully and vigorously. I say not boastfully but somberly, I have not been shy about appointing Independent Counsels when the facts and the law required it. Not a single one of these decisions was the product of an internal poll.

It has been said that I ignored those who advised me to seek the appointment of an Independent Counsel on the theory that a "loose enterprise" may have been at work despite the lack of specific and credible information that a crime may have been committed to justify the appointment of an Independent Counsel. Following that theory loosely would have been inappropriate. There is a grave danger in not adhering to the law's requirement for facts as opposed to rumor, innuendo and speculation. Public officials are not above the law—but they must not be below the law either.

I know you will want to discuss this afternoon several decisions I made under the now defunct Independent Counsel Act.

However difficult and controversial those decisions were and remain today, my decisions under the Act were always—I repeat, always—based on the facts as I understood them and the law as I interpreted it.

I have said before—but it is certainly no less true today—I make the best decisions I can with the information I have at the time. I base my decisions on the facts and the law. I stand by these decisions and the work of the dedicated lawyers in the Department of Justice—whose opinions I value all the more because they are presented to me without fear or favor.

In closing, let me say that while the decisions are mine, the appropriate exercise we are going through is about justice and the Department of Justice—the Department of Justice as an institution that will endure from Administration to Administration through the hard, courageous, and yes, sometimes contentious, work of its dedicated, career employees.

In my confirmation hearing some seven plus years ago now, I told you that I wanted to work with the dedicated men and women at the Department of Justice to establish as hallmarks of that Department, excellence, integrity and professionalism. I look back and say, without ego but with pride, we at the Department have done that. You in the Senate know as well as I, that in the profession of law disagreement is a critical aspect of professionalism; it ensures rigorous analysis and critical thinking on so many important issues.

I am proud of the work that we do at the Department of Justice. And I believe that while we disagree sometimes, on this you and I can agree, that there is a exemplary amount of excellence, professionalism and integrity at the Department of Justice.

Thank you, Mr. Chairman and Members of the Committee. I am happy to respond to your questions.

The CHAIRMAN. Well, thank you, Madam Attorney General.

I will defer to Senator Specter who I believe is going to have 5-minute rounds.

Thank you, Madam Attorney General. I appreciate your appearing. I appreciate you being here.

Attorney General RENO. Thank you, Mr. Chairman.

Senator SPECTER [presiding]. Attorney General Reno, I begin with a memorandum which has been the subject of considerable discussion, and that was from FBI Director Freeh to Mr. Esposito dated December 9, 1996. I will read the pertinent part. "I also advise the Attorney General of Lee Radek's comment to you that there was a lot of 'pressure' on him and on PIS, the Public Integrity Section, regarding this case because 'the Attorney General's job might hang in the balance' (or words to that effect)." I stated those comments would be enough for me to take him and the Criminal Division off the case completely.

Did Director Freeh say that to you, Attorney General Reno?

Attorney General RENO. I don't have any recollection of it, Senator. What I have in terms of a recollection of the things that he covers in the whole memo is his reference at a time and place different than he suggests that this meeting took place in which he talked about the need for a junkyard dog prosecutor and that he was anxious to have the matter referred to the FBI, but I am sure he thinks he said it in those words or in so many other words, but I don't remember it, sir.

Senator SPECTER. Well, in this memo, he talks about the junkyard dog concept, but I come back to this point, Attorney General Reno, because it is a very unusual point to refer to one of your top deputies, Mr. Radek, talking about pressure on him and on his unit, with the Attorney General's job might hang in the balance. If in fact that was said, isn't that something of sufficient importance that you would remember?

Attorney General RENO. Yes, I think so, sir, but I think Director Freeh—I feel very strongly that he thinks he said it. I don't know how he said it or the circumstances that occurred at that moment, but I have no memory of it, and clearly, if I had had any memory of it, I would have gone back to Lee Radek and said, "What is this all about?"

Senator SPECTER. But you think that if it had been said, you would remember it?

Attorney General RENO. I think if I had understood it, I would have remembered it. I think he said it, or thinks that he said it, in that or so many other words, and it's the so many other words and so many other words that is the puzzle to me of what I might have confused. I note that Neil Gallagher said that there was pressure to do a good job because it was going to be a critical and sensitive investigation.

Senator SPECTER. Neil Gallagher and Mr. Esposito confirmed that Mr. Radek did say that.

Attorney General RENO. I understand that, and that is what——

Senator SPECTER. Of course, they were not present.

Attorney General RENO. That was what was confusing to me that they talk about the pressure to do a good job. I don't know how Director Freeh said it, but I did not understand it.

Senator SPECTER. Let me move to another subject because the time is very short.

I quote very briefly from your testimony on confirmation about the need for independent counsel where you said, "It is absolutely essential for the public to have confidence in the system, and you cannot do that when there is a conflict or an appearance of conflict in the person who in effect is the chief prosecutor. The credibility and public confidence engendered with the fact that an independent and impartial outsider has examined the evidence and concluded that prosecution is not warranted serves to clear a public official's name in a way that no Justice Department investigation ever could."

Now, I have recited key facts as to the Vice President, and there have been references made to Cisneros and Espy. I turn now to Alexis Herman where you appointed the independent counsel, but in your submission said, "While I cannot conclusively determine at this time that any of these allegations are credible, much of the detail of the story he has told has been corroborated, though none of it clearly inculpates Herman. Although our investigation has developed no evidence clearly demonstrating Secretary Herman's involvement in these matters and substantial evidence suggesting that she may not have been involved, a great deal of Yahni's story has been corroborated. We are, thus, unable to conclude that it is not credible."

Now, it is true that asking for independent counsel means that you have to make a determination.

A red light went on. I will finish within 30 seconds.

You must make a determination that there are reasonable grounds to believe that further investigation is warranted. We are not saying that the Vice President committed perjury, as Senator Torricelli has raised the question, but only of sufficient evidence to go further. In light of what is on the record to the Vice President, how can you order independent counsel for Alexis Herman, but not for Vice President Gore?

Attorney General RENO. First of all, I did not order an independent counsel. I don't have that power. The court——

Senator SPECTER. Recommended it.

Attorney General RENO. I apply to the court, and the court appoints.

In that instance, I have got to trigger a preliminary investigation, if I can, on two accounts: one, if I have specific and credible information that a crime may have been committed; or, two, if I cannot show that the information was either specific and credible or that I can disprove it. So that is what precipitated the triggering of the preliminary investigation in Secretary Herman's case.

In the course of the investigation, I could not disprove or I could not prove that he was not credible, and, thus, felt that the further investigation was necessary because I, under the Independent Counsel Act while conducting a preliminary investigation, did not have the tools to get to the answer that was—such as a grand jury proceeding, subpoenas, or immunity issues.

In the instance of the Vice President, you have spoken of poor people who remembered. Mr. Strauss did not remember. When shown his notes, he said that must have been the case, but he had no memory. We interviewed 15 people, two of whom remembered the discussion. The wide variety of—and everybody gave information. Nobody seemed to withhold information. And we could not, as we spell out in the submission to the court, which has been a matter of public record, which is a very careful report on just what we did. As noted above, in order to prove a violation of Section 1001 in this case, the Government would have to prove beyond a reasonable doubt that at the time he made the telephone calls that were at issue in the '97 investigation, the Vice President actually knew that the media campaign had a hard money component or that the limit on hard money was $20,000. In this case, there is no direct evidence of such knowledge. While the Vice President was present at the meeting, there is no evidence that he heard the statements or understood their implications so as to suggest the falsity of his statements 2 years later that he believed the media fund was entirely soft money, nor does anyone recall the Vice President asking any questions or making any comments at the meeting about the media fund, much less questions or comments indicating an understanding of the issues of the blend of hard and soft money needed for DNC media expenditures.

Witnesses were also asked whether they recalled any other discussion with the Vice President about the hard money component of the media fund. None recalled any, nor did any recall the Vice President saying or doing anything at any other time that would indicate that indeed he knew, whether from the meeting or some other source, that there was a hard money component to the media fund.

I would ask each of you, I would ask everybody listening, if you had a meeting—if you had a meeting 2 years before of this committee and somebody raised a subject and you did not hear it or do not remember it, can you be expected to remember everything you hear at every meeting you go to? And what we concluded in this instance was that the range of impressions and vague misunderstandings among all the meeting attendees is striking and undercuts any reasonable inference that a mere attendance at the meeting should have served to communicate to the Vice President an accurate understanding of the facts.

We concluded that there was under the law, as the statute spells it out—the statute provides that I shall apply to the division of the court for the appointment of an independent counsel if, upon completion of the preliminary investigation, I determine that there are reasonable grounds to believe that further investigation is warranted. I concluded that there was not.

Let me make sure that—15 attendees were interviewed. The President submitted a statement, and one other attendee has testified about the meeting under oath saying he had no memory of it.

Senator SPECTER. Thank you.

Senator Leahy.

Senator Torricelli.

Senator TORRICELLI. Thank you, Mr. Chairman.

Madam Attorney General, in reaching judgments about the application of the Independent Counsel Act, it was your practice to consult with a wide range of senior officials in the Justice Department?

Attorney General RENO. That's correct, Senator.

Senator TORRICELLI. And was this a standard list, or did it change on occasion?

Attorney General RENO. It changed, depending on the circumstances, and as people came and left the Department.

Senator TORRICELLI. Mr. Esposito of the FBI testified that actually in this instance he believed that, to your credit, you consulted with a larger group of people, that the FBI had not always been consulted in the past and asked for their advice on independent counsel, but in this instance, given the seriousness of the matter, you seemed to expand the list to get a wider range of opinions.

Attorney General RENO. I included the FBI in my weekly meetings, asking them on each occasion—sometimes the meetings weren't weekly, but they were on the average of about once a week—asking if there was anything else that I should know or argue, did they want to argue with me, did they want to disagree with me. I tried to be as open and as accessible as I could.

Senator TORRICELLI. In the seven other instances when you named an independent counsel, were all of these senior officials in the Justice Department always of a single mind and did they have a single perspective on whether the appointment should be made and on how the Department should proceed, or was it common to have occasionally someone disagree?

Attorney General RENO. I think I made the statement earlier that they were not all unanimous, but I think there were—I would have to go back and look at it, and I am not sure that there were any that were unanimous, but——

Senator TORRICELLI. So it might be unreasonable that this Congress—this committee is questioning the judgment you made because there was not a unanimous consensus among your advisors with regard to a campaign to finance independent counsel, but in fact it was not unusual in the Department for people in other instances, which have received no attention, upon which we have had no hearings, your judgment has not been questions—it was not unusual there for there to be disagreements.

Attorney General RENO. And if you look at the Supreme Court of the United States, 5–4 decisions are often commonplace.

Senator TORRICELLI. In proceeding with the preliminary investigation of the Vice President in 1997 and 1998, the FBI and the Department of Justice interviewed approximately 250 witnesses, including the Vice President, former members of the staff, DNC officials, White House officials, reviewed phone records, interviewed the Vice President personally. In reaching this preliminary inquiry, was this equally exhaustive of the process you went through in other preliminary investigations? It would appear to me that, indeed, you went to some extraordinary lengths that might seem beyond other instances. How would you compare the amount of investigatory work that went into this preliminary inquiry with others that were conducted?

Attorney General RENO. I tried to be as thorough and as complete as I could each time I asked the court for the appointment of an independent counsel or I notified the court that there was no basis for concluding that a further investigation was warranted. So I don't think it was exceptional. We just tried to be thorough in all the instances, Senator.

Senator TORRICELLI. Let me read for you the memoranda, the views of a couple of people, on the central question that Senator Specter raised about whether or not you were under political pressure or some other influence in not naming an independent counsel.

Mr. La Bella in his memorandum writes of discussions with Director Freeh. He repeatedly had assured us and the Congress that while there had been disagreements from time to time over investigative strategy, the investigation had not been impeded or blocked in any way. Mr. La Bella then writes of the task force generally, and Mr. La Bella personally and repeatedly told us that no investigative steps were closed to them, that they were free to follow any leads, and that if their efforts developed specific and credible information that any covered person may have violated the law, the Attorney General would trigger the Act.

Now, it is being alleged by this committee that there was pressure involved or a compromise of judgment, and cited are Mr. La Bella and Mr. Freeh as principal witnesses. I have just read you two statements quoting Mr. La Bella and Mr. Freeh making very clear there was no inappropriate pressure, no other judgments, indeed they tesfify to your own independence of judgment.

Are these statements consistent with what Mr. La Bella and Mr. Freeh told you personally, that while they may have disagreed with your decision, they have never questioned your independence in doing so?

Attorney General RENO. Mr. La Bella sent me a letter that I will treasure that sets forth his feelings, and one of the things that I prize most from these 7 years is something that was given to me by the FBI. It is an Honorary Special Agent badge, and it is something that I treasure. It could not have been given, I think, without Director Freeh's approval. He presented it to me, and he presented it to me after we have had our disagreements, but there is something——

Senator TORRICELLI. Madam Attorney General, you should know that people may have the impression that those who disagreed with you on the independent counsel statute, not only including Mr. Freeh and Mr. La Bella, but indeed the line attorney, Mr. Mansfield and others, that because they disagreed with you, they may believe that you had reached the wrong judgment or that it was not a fair judgment or that the facts only supported a contrary judgment.

In many of our hearings, there have been few of us present, other than the members of the committee itself. So those of us who are joining for the first time today should know this. Not one of them, not one individual who disagreed with you on the appointment of the independent counsel, hesitated to say to this committee that based on the facts and the law, a reasonable person would not have reached the same judgment that you reached.

Finally, if I could, Mr. Chairman—I know the time has expired, and I will then conclude.

Senator SPECTER. Senator Torricelli, we are going to come back for another round. I do not mind your asking another question, but I do not want to establish the precedent that we are going to go to 10-minute rounds here. So I would ask you to wait for the next round.

Senator TORRICELLI. Fine, Mr. Chairman.

The CHAIRMAN. Senator Grassley.

STATEMENT OF HON. CHARLES E. GRASSLEY, A U.S. SENATOR FROM THE STATE OF IOWA

Senator GRASSLEY. Mr. Chairman, I am going to use my time for a statement that the Attorney General can respond to or not respond to, as she likes, during my time on the first round. And then I have some questions I will ask on the second round.

During the course of the Justice Department oversight investigation, my judgment has been that the Justice Department gets mixed reviews. I do not believe the Department deserves the criticism it got for the Wen Ho Lee case. The FISA issue was a close call and other agencies were more responsible for the shortcomings of that case. And that is especially true of the FBI and the Energy Department.

In the Peter Lee case, I believe that was also a close call, and the Navy did a lot to undermine that case. Yes, there was a communication lapse in that case at the Department of Justice, but there was sensitive information involved in that case, the protection of which goes a long way to explaining decisions made in that case.

So that brings us now to the present subject, the campaign fundraising case. Of all of the cases that we have looked at, this is the one which I believe criticism of the Attorney General's position is warranted. We now know that a second attorney, handpicked by the Attorney General to look into the matter, has recommended an outside counsel to investigate the Vice President. The director of the FBI recommended the same, so did the former principal associate deputy AG, Robert Litt.

It seems the Attorney General's judgment to deny the appointment of an outside counsel was based mainly on the arguments of Lee Radek, chief of the Public Integrity Section. Mr. Radek's section has a reputation. The reputation of that office is that it is a big black hole. Mr. Radek is called "Dr. No" by the investigative community because he declines their cases almost automatically. If you are seeking a legal opinion to not do something, just go to Public Integrity. They are a factory with a fast-moving assembly line of negative arguments for prosecution.

I noted at our last hearing that Mr. Radek and the Attorney General changed their legal arguments in midstream about the hard money versus the soft-money issue. First, the argument was that there were no illegalities. Then when the FEC report came out in August 1998 saying there were illegalities, their argument conveniently switched to an advice of counsel argument; in other words, a new argument was needed, so they went to Dr. No for an argument off his assembly line.

You may remember, Mr. Chairman, when Mr. Radek testified in May, we raised a lot of these issues, and they were written about in the newspaper the next day. Later that week in May, the Inspectors General had their monthly meeting, and the issue was raised there. There was a prominent U.S. attorney present in the room who offered up their offices as an alternative to Public Integrity. Some of the Inspectors General vowed to take up the offer and some vowed never to deal with the Public Integrity Section again.

The same concerns about Public Integrity are shared with the U.S. attorney community. I raise this issue to make a point. I cannot believe that the Attorney General and those around her did not know about Public Integrity's reputation and its practices. If I were aware of that reputation, and at the same time getting conflicting arguments from the FBI director, your handpicked attorney of the case, and the principal associate deputy attorney general, I would have thought twice about taking Mr. Radek's advice.

Mr. Chairman, I do commend the Attorney General for an important point, and that is her appearance here. She is here to be accountable, as she always has in these oversight cases. I am sorry to say that the same cannot be said about the FBI director. He has chosen not to come, despite the best efforts of Senator Specter. This committee too often gives the director a pass when he most needs to give an accounting of his input into this decision-making process. We know from documents we have read that he was most emphatic about the need for an independent counsel, and without his appearance there is a colossal void in the context of this hearing and the public's understanding.

I thank you, Mr. Chairman.

The CHAIRMAN. Thank you very much, Senator Grassley.

Senator Leahy.

Attorney General RENO. Could I——

The CHAIRMAN. Yes, of course, you may respond, Attorney General Reno.

Attorney General RENO. Thank you for those comments, and I appreciate it because, Senator Grassley, from the time I first came to make my first courtesy call on you, and you talked to me about Qui Tam, you have always been vigorous and constructive in your discussions, and I appreciate it very much.

One thing I emphatically disagree with you about, and that is Lee Radek. Would that there were more people like Lee Radek in this world. He calls it like he sees it. He has pursued corruption, where U.S. attorneys recuse themselves. He never gets flustered. He tells me exactly what he thinks. I do not always agree with him. But that man is an extraordinary public servant, and he has taken more slings and arrows than anybody deserves, and he is just an extraordinary man. I wish, with all of my heart, Senator, because I think you would appreciate it, that you could sit in the conference room and watch some of these discussions and understand what goes into it. But he is a very special person and a very distinguished public servant.

With respect to us changing our minds, let me tell you precisely the process because it was not a matter of mind changing. Under the Federal Election Campaign Act, for me to prove a case of violation of the act, I must show that it was willful and knowing. The previous administrations had entered into a Memorandum of Understanding with the Federal Elections Commission. Because the standards, particularly with respect to what was an electioneering message which went to the issues advertising, because the Commission, which is responsible under 437 for construing and developing the policy with respect to the Campaign Act, had never developed standards, the issue was we cannot show that it was knowing and willful because we do not know what the standards were.

We knew the Federal Elections Commission was pursuing the issues that had been raised by Common Cause. And when the Federal Elections Commission, we said if they refer it back to us, we will trigger the Independent Counsel Act if they think there was a willful and knowing violation.

Now, the Commission did not act, but the Audit Division acted and concluded that both the Democratic and the Republican candidates, that the issue ads had violated the Campaign Act. At that point, I triggered it. It was not a change of mind or a change of argument.

I went then through a preliminary investigation, as the Independent Counsel Act provides for, and we very carefully reviewed it. The defense was what did the lawyers say? And the finding that we spell out here is very detailed, shows the great lengths we went to. It is 31 pages. It goes into great detail as to how we went through the process. And if somebody relies, in good faith, on advice of counsel, I cannot show, and no reasonable investigation could further show that that advice and reliance was not warranted. So that is where we ended up. It was not a change of mind. It was trying to use the MOU that had existed from one administration to another and the investigation to take us to where we are at.

The CHAIRMAN. Senator Leahy.

Senator LEAHY. Mr. Chairman, you know we speak about pressure and who is pressuring who. But in this committee, we have had a member of this committee question a sitting Federal judge about a case, the Peter Lee case, in which the defendant has a motion to terminate his probation.

We publicly urged prosecutors to take certain positions at the upcoming sentencing of Defendant Maria Hsia, even though prosecutors are supposed to be independent. The only interesting thing about that, in that hearing, we had attorneys for both Maria Hsia and the Justice Department here, so they probably both use that public pressure however they want.

We wanted to conduct oversight of the Wen Ho Lee matter, even though an investigation was pending. And now we find that Wen Ho Lee's attorney is asking for our internal documents on that.

Probably the only reason we are not down at the trial in Waco is that, after Republican staffers were sent to Waco to interview witnesses even before Senator Danforth had an opportunity to do so, he angrily told us to butt out.

So let me ask you a couple of direct questions on pressure. Did you ever put pressure on Mr. Radek or anyone else to come out any particular way on any particular matter?

Attorney General RENO. The only thing I ever did to Mr. Radek, I think, was to tell him that I wanted to make sure that campaign financing cases that were in the U.S. Attorney's Offices were brought to Washington so that we could review them to make sure that we were consistent in our approaches. And he objected, and I said I thought we should.

Senator LEAHY. Did you ask him to come out a certain way, though, in determining which way, whether to prosecute or not to prosecute on those campaign finance cases?

Attorney General RENO. Never.

Senator LEAHY. Did the President——

Attorney General RENO. And if I had told him to, he would have told me to take a flying leap.

Senator LEAHY. I am sure he would have. I know him.

Did the President of the United States ever pressure you to come out a particular way on any particular matter?

Attorney General RENO. No, sir.

Senator LEAHY. Did the Vice President of the United States ever pressure you to come out a particular way on a particular matter?

Attorney General RENO. No, sir.

Senator LEAHY. We do know that in the Senate, the Senate Republicans have been calling for an appointment of an independent counsel since at least March 1997, when they passed the Senate resolution to that effect even before the facts came out. Is it safe to say, however, you do not take pressure here either?

Attorney General RENO. I always try to listen and learn.

Senator LEAHY. Not quite the question, but I think we both know the answer.

Can you remember of things 2 years ago? Some of us sometimes have a little trouble remembering 2 hours ago. But I know some have criticized the fact that the Vice President submitted a statement, following an interview with FBI and task force investigators, to clarify some of his answers relating to coffees. Well, FBI Director Freeh testified before a House appropriations subcommittee recently, he then sent a statement clarifying certain of his answers. And, in fact, we encourage witnesses before this committee, once they have read the transcript, if they want to clarify something, they should do it.

Some have claimed that the Vice President must have known the media fund, which was the subject of the disputed telephone calls, had a hard-money component because there was a memorandum written by somebody to the Vice President. That is basically the same thing when Director Freeh let the subcommittee know in the House, "Well, there is a memorandum here which I had not seen. I want to add to my understanding." That certainly would not suggest anything wrong on his part, would it?

Attorney General RENO. No, sir.

Senator LEAHY. And is it possible to assume that not all of us in public office read every single item put before us?

Attorney General RENO. I think there are too many trees that have been cut down to permit us to do that.

Senator LEAHY. And DOJ I think has a policy declining to prosecute violations of these minor matters, the de minimus matters. In fact, in 1976, the Justice Department declined to prosecute officials responsible for sending letters signed by President Ford to Federal employees at their workplaces, soliciting contributions for Republican congressional candidates. In 1988, prosecution was declined when two Republican Senators, one still serving, sent solicitation—in fact, is serving as a member of this committee—sent solicitation as part of a computerized direct mailing to employees of the Criminal Division of DOJ. Would you not say they probably did just the right thing to ignore those?

Attorney General RENO. Yes, sir.

Senator LEAHY. And in the Buddhist Temple, we should note if this was a democratic fundraiser and was expected to be, I am sure that Vice President Gore was probably very surprised to see a number of Republican elected officials who were there. And that may be one reason why he might not have thought it was a fundraiser, when the Republicans, elected Republicans, were present at that event.

Thank you, Mr. Chairman

The CHAIRMAN. Senator Kyl.

Senator KYL. Thank you, Mr. Chairman.

Senator Leahy, I am proud to say that there are elected Democrat officeholders at some of my fundraisers.

Senator LEAHY. You never invited me.

Senator KYL. I did not invite you. That is right. But when you are ready to contribute, let me know.

Madam Attorney General, I wanted to ask you, first, about the "willful and knowing" standard, as it pertained to the Vice President's knowledge or lack of knowledge about the fundraising constituting or including hard-money fundraising.

You said, as I recall, that his mere attendance at meetings was not enough to conclude that the Vice President knew that hard money was involved; is that correct? Words to that effect?

Attorney General RENO. We go into great detail, sir, but that is generally correct.

Senator KYL. Obviously, it can be that records and other witnesses' testimony can rebut a single person's denial.

Attorney General RENO. That is correct. And we were seeking to determine whether there was any evidence from which one might reasonably infer that the Vice President actually knew. It might be supported, for example, by other attendees who might specifically recall something. We pursued each and developed no information.

Senator KYL. Well, that is exactly what I wanted to ask you. What other evidence did you consider that may have suggested that the Vice President knew or should have known that hard money was involved?

Attorney General RENO. Such an inference might be supported, for example, by information that these facts were discussed in sufficient detail and focus at the meeting that many other attendees specifically recall them, that the Vice President made comments or asked questions in the course of the discussion that would seem to reflect an active understanding of the details, that the participants recalled any affirmative discussion of a need to raise hard money for the media fund, that the Vice President read memoranda that made these points or that anyone spoke directly to the Vice President on any occasion about the need to raise hard money.

Senator KYL. And was there not evidence to support some of those possibilities?

Attorney General RENO. We found none.

Senator KYL. None at all?

Attorney General RENO. No, sir.

Senator KYL. There was no one who recalled a discussion of hard money at those meetings?

Attorney General RENO. As I told you previously, there were two.

Senator KYL. So the answer was not that there was none, but that there was some, but that you did not consider it sufficient.

Attorney General RENO. What I said was that we did not have any information that these facts were discussed in sufficient detail and focus at the meeting that many other attendees specifically recall them. And 15 individuals, including the President and Vice President, attended the meeting. All 15 were interviewed, with two exceptions: one, who testified under oath in the course of a congressional investigation that he had no recollection of the meeting, and that if he attended at all, he likely would have left after just a few minutes; and the President, who provided us with a statement that he had no independent recollection of the meeting.

Senator KYL. Did any of the witnesses testify that they recalled hard money being discussed at these meetings?

Attorney General RENO. No attendees recall any particular questions or comments by the Vice President; two recall——

Senator KYL. Well, that—I am sorry—that was not my question.

Attorney General RENO. Only two of the fifteen attendees at the meeting even recall the topic of a hard-money component to the media fund being raised during the meeting. While the author of the notes had no specific recollection of the meeting, he did confirm, based on his habit and practice, his belief that the words noted in his handwriting were things said during the meeting, that he recorded them as they were said.

Senator KYL. Were there any other memoranda that you believe came to the attention of the Vice President that suggested that hard money was involved?

Attorney General RENO. The issue was raised previously, as I recall, about the Ickes memorandum. Six or seven of the memoranda were received before the telephone calls were made. The remainder were made afterwards.

Senator KYL. Rather than asking you to recall each of those, Madam Attorney General, since I have just one other quick question, would you be willing to submit, at this point in the record, the evidence that was considered, but deemed insufficient, to supply the "willful and knowing" attribution to the Vice President?

Attorney General RENO. I trust it is a matter of record with the committee. It has been public record for some time, and it is the notification that we filed with the Court on this issue. The first, with respect to the first matter, it was 29 pages in length, and I believe 19 pages in length for the second matter.

Senator KYL. Would you then simply just direct the committee's attention to the points where that specific evidence is?

Attorney General RENO. Yes, I can do that right now.

Senator KYL. Well, no, if I might, while I still have just a moment, if you would just do that for the record, that will be sufficient for my purposes.

Attorney General RENO. Yes, sir.

[The information follows:]

UNITED STATES COURT OF APPEALS
FOR THE DISTRICT OF COLUMBIA CIRCUIT

Division for the Purpose of
Appointing Independent Counsels

Ethics in Government Act of 1978, As Amended

In re: Albert Gore, Jr.

Before: SENTELLE, *Presiding Judge*, BUTZNER and FAY, *Senior Circuit Judges*

Order Authorizing Attorney General to Disclose
Notification of Results of Preliminary Investigation

Upon consideration of the request of the Attorney General pursuant to 28 U.S.C. § 592(e) for authorization to disclose the Notification to the Court Pursuant to § 592(b) of Results of Preliminary Investigation in this matter, which concerns allegations that have been widely reported by the news media, it is hereby

ORDERED, in the public interest that leave is granted to the Attorney General pursuant to 28 U.S.C. § 592(e) to publicly disclose the Notification.

Per Curiam:
For the Court:

Mark J. Langer, Clerk

by

Marilyn R. Sargent
Chief Deputy Clerk

DOJ-02666

UNITED STATES COURT OF APPEALS
FOR THE DISTRICT OF COLUMBIA CIRCUIT
INDEPENDENT COUNSEL DIVISION

United States Court of Appeals
For the District of Columbia Circuit

FILED DEC 02 1997

In re ALBERT GORE, JR.   )
)   No.
)

Special Division

. . . .

NOTIFICATION TO THE COURT PURSUANT TO 28 U.S.C. § 592(b) OF RESULTS OF PRELIMINARY INVESTIGATION

On October 3, 1997, I notified this Court of the initiation of a preliminary investigation of Vice President of the United States Albert Gore, Jr. The preliminary investigation has now been concluded, and I have determined that there are no reasonable grounds to believe that further investigation is warranted of allegations that the Vice President violated federal law, 18 U.S.C. § 607, by making fundraising telephone calls from his office in the White House. My conclusion is supported by two independent dispositive grounds. First, the evidence that the Vice President may have violated section 607 is insufficient to warrant further investigation. Second, even if the evidence suggested a possible violation of law, established Department of Justice policy requires that there be aggravating circumstances before a prosecution of a section 607 violation is warranted. There is no evidence of any aggravating circumstances in this matter. Therefore, appointment of an independent counsel is not being sought. In accordance with the requirements of 28 U.S.C. § 592(b), this notification will summarize the information received and the results of the preliminary investigation.

2

INFORMATION RECEIVED

On September 3, 1997, the Washington Post reported that records made available by the White House revealed that more than $120,000 in contributions solicited over the telephone by the Vice President from his White House office were deposited into the Democratic National Committee's (DNC's) federal account. The article named six individuals who, in a period from November 1995 through April 1996, made a donation to the DNC soon after they may have received a call from the Vice President. The Post further reported that the DNC deposited a portion of each gift made by these persons into a federal or "hard money" account and deposited the remainder into a non-federal "soft money" account. The Post also reported that the DNC had reimbursed the United States Treasury in the amount of $24.20 for fundraising telephone calls apparently made from the Vice President's office.[1]

The article thus suggested that the Vice President may have violated federal law by making fundraising solicitation calls from his White House office which resulted in hard money contributions. This is a potential violation of 18 U.S.C. § 607, which criminalizes the solicitation of contributions within the meaning of the Federal Election Campaign Act (FECA), or so-called hard or federal contributions, in the federal work space.

---

[1] Some have suggested that the fact that a few of the telephone calls were initially billed to the federal government might amount to a technical and temporary "conversion" of federal property. However, it is the established practice of the Department of Justice not to investigate or prosecute such minor allegations, and this matter will not be pursued. See, 28 U.S.C. § 592(c)(1)(B).

3

After I received confirmation that Federal Election Commission (FEC) records reflected federal contributions by the donors named in the *Post* article around the time of the alleged solicitations by the Vice President, I commenced a 30-day initial inquiry under the Independent Counsel Act. My decision at that time was premised on the plausible inference that if a donor had contributed hard money to the DNC in response to a solicitation by the Vice President, the Vice President may have asked the donor to make a hard money contribution. On October 3, 1997, I commenced a preliminary investigation in accordance with the requirements of the Independent Counsel Act.

APPLICABLE LAW

First enacted in 1883 as part of the Pendleton Act, section 607 provides in relevant part:

> (a) It shall be unlawful for any person to solicit or receive any contribution within the meaning of section 301(8) of the Federal Election Campaign Act of 1971 in any room or building occupied in the discharge of official duties by any person mentioned in section 603, or in any navy yard, fort, or arsenal. Any person who violates this section shall be fined under this title or imprisoned not more than three years, or both.[2]

---

[2] A significant open legal issue under section 607 is whether a telephone call solicitation *from* federal work space *to* a private location is a solicitation "in" the federal work space. This is a difficult legal issue made more complicated by the legislative history of section 607 and by the only Supreme Court decision discussing the statute, United States v. Thaver, 209 U.S. 39 (1908). Thaver held that a letter written and sent from outside federal work space, but delivered to an individual in a federal office, violates section 607. In so holding, the Court concluded that "the solicitation was in the place where the letter was received," id. at 44, language which clearly could be read to suggest that a solicitation received outside the federal workplace does not occur "in" the federal workplace.

4

The concept of hard as opposed to soft money in the context of federal election law is important to an understanding of this matter. The phrase "hard money" is a colloquial phrase commonly used to refer to "contributions" within the meaning of section 301(8) of the Federal Election Campaign Act (FECA). Section 301(8) of the FECA defines a "contribution" as "any gift ... made by any person for the purpose of influencing any election for Federal office." 2 U.S.C. § 431(8)(A)(i). Because the term is defined in terms of an intent to influence a _federal_ campaign, hard money is also often referred to as "federal" money, and the political parties maintain separate bank accounts, called federal and non-federal accounts, to keep the two kinds of donations separate. As can be seen from the language of section 607 set out above, a violation of that statute specifically requires a solicitation of hard money.

The FECA sets out various limitations on how much individuals can contribute in hard money. Of particular significance to this matter is the limitation on donations to national political committees, such as the DNC; individuals can contribute up to $20,000 in hard money to a national political

---

While the facts of _Thayer_ are distinguishable from those here, the legal obstacle created by the _Thayer_ decision would be a formidable barrier to any prosecution based on these facts. However, I have concluded based on the clear facts developed in the course of this preliminary investigation that I need not finally resolve this legal issue. Therefore, I have assumed for purposes of this investigation that under section 607, a solicitation over the telephone could be deemed to have occurred "in" both the location from which the call was placed and the location where the call was received.

5

committee per year. 2 U.S.C. § 441a(a)(1)(B). Corporations and unions are barred from making hard money contributions. 2 U.S.C. § 441b.

"Soft money," in contrast, is commonly understood to refer to all other sorts of political donations to all sorts of political causes. There are no limits under the FECA on the amounts of soft money donations, and soft money donations can be made by corporations and unions, but there are strict limits on the uses to which political parties can put such donations.

SCOPE OF THE INVESTIGATION

The preliminary investigation, which was conducted by attorneys from the Department of Justice and agents of the Federal Bureau of Investigation (FBI), was comprehensive. Approximately 250 witnesses were interviewed. These witnesses included the Vice President, current and former members of the Vice President's staff, other current and former White House officials, officials of the Clinton/Gore '96 Committee (Clinton/Gore '96), various paid and unpaid officers and employees of the DNC, and more than 200 individuals whose names appeared as prospective donors on call sheets prepared by the DNC for the Vice President. Documents were obtained from the White House, the DNC, Clinton/Gore '96, and several of the individuals who received telephone calls from the Vice President.

6

<u>RESULTS OF THE INVESTIGATION</u>

I. <u>The DNC's Media Campaign</u>

Following the 1994 elections, the DNC funded an extensive
series of "issue-oriented" media advertisements. According to
several witnesses, these ads were designed to generate support
for the Clinton Administration's position on various issues and
to frame the debate as the 1996 elections approached.

In a series of memoranda addressed to the President and Vice
President written during 1995 and 1996, then-Deputy White House
Chief of Staff Harold Ickes detailed the way in which the DNC
media campaign was funded throughout this period. Ickes' memos
explain that the ads were paid for during most of this period
with a combination of approximately 60 percent "soft" and 40
percent "hard" money, pursuant to an allocation formula required
by the FEC. This allocation formula reflects the fact that
generic, so-called "issue ads" support and advance the cause of
all party candidates, state and local as well as federal, and
thus need not be paid for entirely from hard money funds. Soft,
or non-federal funds, could be used to pay for a portion of the
advertisements, according to the FEC allocation rules.

II. <u>Inception of 1995-1996 Media Fund Telephone Call Project</u>

The evidence suggests that the topic of fundraising phone
calls for the media campaign was raised during a November 21,
1995 meeting attended by the President, Vice President, several
White House aides, and DNC finance officials. Several memos
written by Ickes and discussed during this meeting show that the

7

media fund, originally budgeted at $10 million for calendar year
1995, was in need of several million dollars to stay afloat
through the end of the year.[3]

The Vice President agreed to, and indeed may have suggested
that he participate in the fundraising effort by making telephone
calls for the DNC media campaign, in part because soliciting by
telephone would be less time-consuming and less tiring than
attending additional fundraising events. None of the witnesses
interviewed recalled any discussion during this period about how
the telephone solicitations would be carried out. Likewise, no
one recalled discussions during this period concerning the
legality or propriety of making these calls from the White House
or the question of whether "hard" or "soft" money would be
solicited.

The evidence suggests that the Vice President, on ten and
perhaps 11 occasions between the fall of 1995 and the spring of
1996, engaged in sessions of telephone calls to raise funds for

---

[3] When shown the Ickes memos that were discussed during the
November 21 meeting, the Vice President stated that as a general
rule he did not read Ickes' memos on DNC finance matters because
the memos usually advocated a position on an issue that invariably
would be discussed at length at a meeting anyway. Thus, the Vice
President explained, he would typically move these memos from his
in-box to his out-box without further review. He added that the
absence of "checkmarks" on any copies of the Ickes documents, often
used by the Vice President to note that he had read a document, is
a further indication that he had not read these documents. Members
of the Vice President's staff confirmed in interviews that the Vice
President often transferred documents from his in-box to his out-
box without having read them, although they did not recall whether
he did so specifically with respect to Ickes' DNC finance memos.

8

the DNC. There is evidence that he spoke to at least 45 people on these occasions.

III. The DNC's Practice of Splitting Contributions

Sometime after the 1994 elections, the DNC, in an effort to maximize its federal or hard money contributions, began a practice of splitting large checks into federal and non-federal components if the donor had not already contributed the maximum $20,000 in hard money to the DNC, and the donor's preference was not made explicit on the contribution check.[4] As a result of this practice, a portion of the contributions from several of the donors solicited by the Vice President was deposited into federal accounts. We were told that under DNC procedure, after the contribution was split the donor was supposed to be notified by letter of the fact that a portion of the contribution was being treated as a hard money contribution. If the donor approved the allocation, the funds would stay in the federal account.

However, the DNC failed to send the notification letters from late 1995 through the first half of 1996. As a result, portions of several of the contributions solicited by the Vice President remained in federal accounts and were reported to the FEC as hard money contributions without the donors' knowledge or consent.

---

[4] Prior to this, when DNC fundraisers had wanted to raise large donations, they typically had asked donors to provide two checks, one up to $20,000 for the federal portion, and the other for the remaining amount to be deposited into a non-federal account.

In the course of the investigation, agents and prosecutors interviewed all current and former DNC finance and accounting employees who could be identified as having any familiarity with the DNC's practice of splitting donations and depositing a portion into hard money accounts. None of these witnesses stated that they had any knowledge or information that the Vice President -- or anyone else in the White House -- was aware of the DNC's practice of allocating funds into hard money accounts.[5]

The funding of the DNC media campaign was discussed in a February 22, 1996, memorandum from Harold Ickes addressed to the President and the Vice President, and an attached memorandum written by DNC Chief Financial Officer Bradley Marshall, dated February 21, 1996. The Marshall memo, in the context of detailing a current shortage of non-federal money, states:

> I understand that Finance has raised and is currently processing, $1.2 million. At this point, I do not know how it will breakdown between Federal vs Non-Federal and Corporate vs Individual.

In what may be a reference to this "breakdown," Marshall adds the following information three paragraphs later:

> Definition of Federal and Non-Federal monies (from the DNC perspective):
>
> Federal money is the first $20,000 given by an individual, ($40,000 from a married couple). Any amount over this $20,000 amount from an individual is

---

[5] Of these current and former DNC employees, only Chief Financial Officer Bradley Marshall ever had dealings with White House personnel. Marshall does not recall ever discussing the DNC's allocation practice with any members of the White House staff.

considered Non-Federal Individual. An individual can give an unlimited amount of Non-Federal Individual money.

While the Marshall memorandum could be read by one who knew of the practice of splitting contributions as reflecting that practice, there is no explicit reference to the practice in the memorandum. It is my conclusion that the memorandum, standing alone and without independent knowledge of the splitting practice, cannot reasonably be read as putting anyone on notice that the DNC was engaging in a practice of splitting contributions without the donor's consent. Therefore, even if the Vice President read the Marshall memorandum,[6] it is my conclusion that there is no evidence on which to base a conclusion that the Vice President was aware of the DNC practice, and thus may have been soliciting contributions knowing that a portion of some contributions would end up in hard money accounts.

However, we also attempted to ascertain exactly what the Vice President said in his conversations with the prospective donors, to see whether or not he in fact solicited contributions of hard money.

---

[6] In his interview, the Vice President stated that he was unaware at the time that the DNC was splitting some large contributions and depositing up to $20,000 into its federal account. He does not recall seeing the Marshall memo at the time it apparently was circulated to his office. He believes that he would not have read the Marshall memo because it was attached to an Ickes memo discussing DNC finance matters, which the Vice President says he generally did not read.

11

IV. The Logistics of the Vice President's Solicitations

The preliminary investigation confirmed that, on ten or perhaps 11 occasions beginning in November 1995 and concluding in May 1996, the Vice President made a series of telephone calls from his White House office to private individuals seeking their financial support for the DNC media campaign. These sessions followed a pattern. A "call sheet" containing information about the prospective donor and his or her contribution history was prepared by a member of the DNC Finance staff and delivered to Peter Knight. Knight, who had headed the Vice President's staff when the Vice President served in the House of Representatives and the Senate, sat in on several of the Vice President's telephone sessions; other staff members sat in on the remainder of the sessions. The preliminary investigation developed substantial undisputed evidence that the telephone calls were in fact placed from the Vice President's office in the White House.

V. The Contents of the Solicitations

A total of 216 prospective donors was identified from call sheets and lists prepared for the Vice President by the DNC and obtained by the FBI in the course of the preliminary investigation. The FBI interviewed or received statements from well over 200 of these individuals.[7] Of these, 159 did not

---

[7] I do not believe that the fact that a handful of individuals declined to be interviewed requires that appointment of an independent counsel be sought. Only eight individuals for whom there were call sheets declined to be interviewed. The consistency of the investigative results and the strong evidence that the Vice President was affirmatively soliciting soft money contributions renders any hypothetical possibility that one of

recall receiving a telephone call regarding political contributions from the Vice President.[8] Forty-five people recalled having had telephone conversations about political contributions with the Vice President in either late 1995 or early to mid-1996.[9]

A. The Donations Deposited into Federal Accounts. The evidence suggests that five of these 45 prospective donors were solicited by the Vice President, and gave a donation that was subsequently deposited, in part, into the DNC's federal account without their knowledge. Another 12 provided contributions to the DNC that were deposited entirely into a non-federal account.

---

these additional individuals may have been solicited for hard money pure speculation. In addition, as to three of these individuals, other than the existence of a call sheet, there is no evidence that they were ever called, and it should be recalled that there are scores of call sheets as to which no solicitation call was ever made. As to three others, there are no donations, hard or soft, at the time of the calls. Finally, as to the last two individuals, documentary evidence in the form of contemporaneous notes of the conversation on the call sheets affirmatively suggests that they were solicited for a soft money contribution, although neither of the two made a donation at the time of the call.

[8] In spite of these recollections, there is some documentary evidence suggesting that the Vice President may have called a handful of these people at some point. Nevertheless, we have found no evidence that the Vice President asked for federal contributions or that hard money contributions were given in response to a solicitation, if indeed one was made.

[9] In addition, four individuals recalled receiving telephone solicitations from the Vice President in the Fall of 1994. According to both the Vice President and former DNC Finance official Terry McAuliffe, the Vice President made those calls while on a visit to the DNC to boost staff morale immediately prior to the 1994 elections. Those solicitations raise no questions of impropriety under section 607 because they were not made from federal office space.

13

to give. The remaining nineteen remember the purpose of the Vice President's call as a thank you, rather than as a solicitation.[10] None of these 45 persons stated that the Vice President explicitly or implicitly asked them to give money to the DNC's federal account or to any federal political campaign. This is consistent with the Vice President's statement in his interview that he believed at the time that, in all instances, he was asking prospective donors to make soft money contributions to the DNC to fund the DNC's issue-oriented media campaign.

The preliminary investigation definitively established that the Vice President made four telephone solicitations from the White House which resulted in donors contributing funds to the DNC that were thereafter deposited into a DNC hard money account. A fifth such solicitation was suggested by circumstantial evidence.[11] All five of these donors were interviewed in the course of the investigation. Four of the five specifically described the Vice President's solicitation as having been for a contribution to the "DNC media fund" or more generically to fund

---

[10]   Given the elements of section 607, it is clear that a prosecution could not be based on a call to thank a donor for a previous commitment to make a contribution. Section 607 does not restrict the Vice President generally from engaging in conduct relating to political fundraising. Rather, it specifically criminalizes only soliciting federal contributions in the federal workplace. One cannot "solicit" something that has already been provided or agreed to.

[11] The difference between this number and the number originally reported in the Post article can be traced to the fact that the Post relied largely on call sheets to support its allegations, rather than interviews with all the donors.

a DNC advertising campaign, rather than for a contribution to the DNC federal account or to any candidate for federal office.

The fifth donor remembers a telephone call from the Vice President, though he does not recall a solicitation in the course of the conversation. He did make a subsequent donation to the DNC; however, he links his donation to later conversations with a high-level Democratic fundraiser, rather than to his conversation with the Vice President.

It is my view that there are no further grounds to investigate whether any of these calls violated section 607 on the mere grounds that a portion of the subsequent contributions was deposited into hard money accounts. There is no evidence that the Vice President was aware that part of the donations would be deposited into hard money accounts, and the donors' own descriptions of the solicitations makes it clear that they interpreted the solicitations as being for soft money.

B. The Substance of the Solicitations. The above-described investigation disposed of the original inference on which this preliminary investigation was based, that if a donor made a contribution deposited into a hard money account, it is reasonable to infer that he or she may have been solicited for a hard money contribution. However, we recognized that this did not fully dispose of the possibility that the Vice President may have solicited hard money contributions in the course of his telephone calls. In response to a request for a hard money contribution, a donor may have declined to give a hard money

contribution, perhaps having reached his or her maximum for the
year, but agreed nevertheless to make a soft money donation. Or
a prospective donor may have declined altogether following the
solicitation. Based on this possibility, it was determined that
the preliminary investigation should seek as comprehensive a
review as possible of the Vice President's solicitation calls.

Setting aside the five contributions which were deposited
into hard money accounts, which, as I have explained above, the
evidence shows occurred without the knowledge of the Vice
President, the evidence that the Vice President may have
solicited hard money contributions is slight indeed. The sum
total of the evidence that the Vice President may have sought
hard money contributions from donors consists of two passing and
largely ambiguous comments concerning elections to potential
donors, one assumption made by a donor, and a set of
circumstances regarding another, involving four solicitations out
of a total of 45, an ambiguous note jotted on one call sheet, and
the fact that many of the Vice President's calls, although they
were made on behalf of the DNC, were charged to a Clinton/Gore
campaign credit card:

1)   There is evidence that one potential donor assumed the
Vice President was talking about a campaign contribution.
However, he states that he believes that at the time he may not
have known about the difference between hard and soft money. His
only recollection of what the Vice President said was "any help
you can give would be appreciated." Nothing in this vague

16

request could be pointed to as evidence that the Vice President
was soliciting hard rather than soft money. Furthermore, the
Vice President's initial broaching of the subject was immediately
followed by a declination from the potential donor, and the Vice
President dropped the subject, so there is no additional context
from which it could reasonably be inferred that the solicitation
was for hard money. This exchange does not reasonably suggest
that the Vice President was soliciting hard money, and there is
no conceivable additional investigation that could develop proof
that that is what occurred.

2) There is evidence that in the course of one
conversation, the Vice President mentioned facing a "tough
election." While the donor recalls this remark, he also recalls
that the Vice President specifically requested funds to help get
the DNC message out on issues such as health care. This issue-
oriented request, together with the fact that the request was for
$30,000, strongly supports the position that the specific request
made was intended to be for soft money. Furthermore, the donor
affirmatively understood the request as being for soft money.

3) In a third conversation, the Vice President mentioned
that previous elections had not gone well. He made no reference
to a contribution for any future election, but rather said that a
media campaign was needed to promote "Democratic issues." The
donor believed that the solicitation was for soft money, because
the request was for support of "issue oriented ads," which could
be paid for with soft money. Furthermore, the amount of the

be paid for with soft money. Furthermore, the amount of the request was such that the Vice President was necessarily asking for at least some soft money, and there was no mention in the conversation that would support the notion that he was requesting any hard money.

4) There is evidence that one potential donor attended a party meeting, also attended by the Vice President, at which proposed television issue-oriented ads were aired for party supporters, and at which it was observed that the ads were proving effective in building support for the President's reelection effort. Subsequently, when the Vice President called the potential donor, he specifically requested support for the DNC's media campaign, making reference to the prior meeting.

This final solicitation was, again, a solicitation to support the media campaign. The fact that the donor was told several weeks earlier that the media campaign would also support the President's reelection adds nothing of substance. It is true that the ad campaign would support, in part, the President's reelection, but that fact is accounted for under the law by the fact that hard money must be used in part to pay for the advertisements. The fact that this reality had been previously brought to the donor's attention does not support an inference that a later general request from the Vice President for support

18

for the media campaign was a request for hard rather than soft
money.[12]

5) On the call sheet for a fifth prospective donor, there
is a notation "no federal $ '95." The donor was called in late
1995, and thus it could be argued that the inference to be drawn
from the notation was that he should be asked for a hard money
contribution. However, this donor has a clear recollection and
contemporaneous notes of his conversation with the Vice President
which conclusively establish that he was solicited for a soft
money contribution, which he in fact made. Most compellingly,
his notes indicate that he asked the Vice President how he should
make out his check, and he was specifically told to make it out
to a DNC non-federal account.

6) Finally, many of the Vice President's calls were charged
to a Clinton/Gore campaign calling card, rather than to a DNC
calling card. This, it could be argued, suggests an inference

---

[12] The fact that legal soft money expenditures play a role
in federal elections has been expressly acknowledged by the FEC.
In one publication, the FEC pointed out that "most of the soft
money spending that benefits federal candidates occurs when a
committee simultaneously supports both federal and nonfederal
candidates. Party committees, for example, may purchase generic
get-out-the-vote advertisements that benefit both their federal
and nonfederal candidates. To pay for these ads, committees must
use federal funds for the portion that benefits federal
candidates, but may use soft money for the rest." Federal
Election Commission, The Presidential Public Funding Program 22
(1993) The FEC went on to acknowledge in the same publication
that "[f]unds not subject to the federal election law ("soft
money") may also play a role in Presidential elections." Id. at
30.

19

that the Vice President was soliciting hard money campaign
contributions, rather than soft money support for the DNC.

The Vice President stated that at the time, his concern was
that the calls not be charged to the government, and he sought
and received assurance from his assistant that they were being
charged to a calling card. He states that he was not aware at
the time that a campaign calling card had been issued to him or
that his assistant had obtained such a card. None of the other
witnesses involved in the logistics of setting up the telephone
calls had any information that the Vice President had any
knowledge of what particular card was being used. In any event,
whatever inference might be drawn from the fact that a campaign
calling card was used, our investigation explored the
solicitations themselves, and developed no evidence that the Vice
President ever solicited hard money campaign contributions.

My analysis of each of the foregoing telephone calls leads
to a conclusion that none, standing alone or taken together,
support a conclusion that the Vice President was soliciting hard
money contributions when he made the fundraising telephone calls.
In addition, there is a wealth of affirmative evidence gathered
in the course of the preliminary investigation demonstrating that
the Vice President was not soliciting hard money, and thus
supporting my conclusion that no further investigation is
warranted:

1) As noted above, there is no evidence that the Vice
President knew of the DNC practice of reallocating a portion of

20

large contributions to hard money accounts. Nor is there any
reason to believe that further investigation would uncover such
evidence.

2) There is no evidence that the Vice President asked any of
the individuals he contacted directly for funds to support his
reelection or the election of any other federal official.

3) There is affirmative evidence that the Vice President
asked for support for the DNC media campaign in virtually every
call.

4) All donors who understood the concepts of hard and soft
money, and who had an affirmative impression of what was being
requested, believed it was a solicitation for soft money.

5) In several conversations with donors who understood the
difference between hard and soft money contributions, the
discussion explicitly focussed on the fact that the Vice
President was soliciting soft money.

6) In the vast majority of the cases, donations resulting
from the Vice President's solicitations were handled by the DNC
as soft money. In the few cases where they were not, the
evidence suggests that this was done without the donors' or the
Vice President's knowledge.

7) The amounts of money requested in every case, and the
fact that the evidence suggests that corporate support was
expressly solicited in several cases, suggest prima facie that
the requests were for soft money. Hard money donations in those
amounts or from corporate or union sources would have been

unlawful. There is no evidence to suggest that there was ever any discussion or understanding by either the Vice President or any of the donors that a portion of any donation might be treated as hard money.

8) Finally, the Vice President provided a reasonable explanation for his conduct. He stated that he understood the media campaign to be funded entirely by soft money, and that he was soliciting large soft money contributions specifically for that campaign. While his understanding of how the media campaign was funded was not correct, nothing developed in the course of the preliminary investigation contradicts that this was his understanding.

PROSECUTION POLICIES OF THE DEPARTMENT OF JUSTICE

Even if the evidence in this matter were sufficient to suggest that the Vice President may have violated section 607 when he made fundraising telephone calls from his office in the White House, I am required to consider Justice Department policies in determining whether further investigation is warranted under the Independent Counsel Act.

The Act provides:

> In determining whether reasonable grounds exist to warrant further investigation, the Attorney General shall comply with the written or other established policies of the Department of Justice with respect to the conduct of criminal investigations.

28 U.S.C. § 592(c)(1)(B). Congress first added this provision to the Act when it was reauthorized in 1983, when it became clear that the strict procedures of the Act had created a disparity in

the law, subjecting covered persons to investigation and
potential prosecution in situations the Department of Justice
would not ordinarily pursue. See S. Rep. No. 496, 97th Cong.,
2d Sess. 1 (1982), reprinted in 1982 U.S.C.C.A.N. 3537.
Specifically, Congress recognized that the prior law "create[d]
unfairness by imposing a stricter application of criminal law on
public officials than that imposed on private citizens." 1982
U.S.C.C.A.N. at 3548. This stricter application resulted in part
because the low threshold of the prior law could "trigger[] the
appointment of a special prosecutor to investigate allegations
which are not ordinarily prosecuted by the Department of
Justice." Id. at 3550.

The Senate Report makes the intent of Congress explicit:

> Requiring appointment of a special prosecutor to investigate
> alleged violations in instances where a clear Departmental
> policy not to prosecute exists is inconsistent with the
> Act's goal of establishing a standard administration of
> justice for officials and non-officials. Instead, it
> creates unfairness by imposing a stricter application of
> criminal law on public officials.

Id. at 3551.

In 1987, following two decisions by the Attorney General
that closed independent counsel matters without seeking
appointment of an independent counsel, based on a conclusion by
the Attorney General that the cases presented no reasonable
prospect of conviction, Congress amended the section to its
present form, to make it clear that the provision was not
intended to permit the Attorney General to make prosecutorial
judgments about the prospects for conviction. Rather, the

provision applies only to established policies that would affect
the need for further investigation of a matter. Congress
reiterated, however, that the basic purpose of the "policy"
provision was "to prevent investigations of government officials
which would not take place if these persons were private
citizens." S. Rep. No. 123, 100th Cong., 1st Sess. 2 (1987),
reprinted in 1987 U.S.C.C.A.N. 2150, 2151.

Pursuant to the mandate of this statutory provision, we have
conducted a thorough review of the Department's policies with
respect to section 607. Both the Department's manual, Federal
Prosecution of Election Offenses, and a lengthy series of
memoranda prepared by the Department resolving specific cases
brought to our attention over the years were reviewed. Based
upon the results of this review, it is clear to me that the
Department has a well-established policy of declining prosecution
of section 607 violations in the absence of substantial
aggravating factors.[13]

It is telling that while the Department has reviewed scores
of section 607 allegations over the past thirty years, none has

---

[13] I do not find in the record, as some have suggested, that
the Department has a general policy of not prosecuting section
607 violations, in spite of the fact that there have been no such
prosecutions in recent memory. The care with which the Criminal
Division has analyzed numerous allegations under the statute, and
articulated specific reasons warranting not proceeding further,
belies any argument that if a sufficiently aggravated case were
presented, prosecution would not be authorized.

Furthermore, I do not find that coercion is a prerequisite
before prosecution will be considered, although there is some
support for that argument in the documentary record.

24

been judged to warrant prosecution. On the other hand, technical violations, particularly in the context of fundraising letters addressed to federal workers in the workplace, are fairly common, and have been frequently analyzed by the Department.

Public documents reflect the policy that prosecution will only be considered in the presence of aggravating factors.[14] First, in a 1978 letter responding to inquiries from Senator Mark Hatfield about the scope of section 607, then-Assistant Attorney General Patricia Wald acknowledged that the Justice Department's enforcement efforts had historically been "aimed principally" at solicitations directed to federal employees in their offices, rather than at solicitations originating in federal office space. She explained that:

> This enforcement pattern is a product of the tendency of the former situation to present more aggravation than the latter. However, we believe that Section 60[7] can be

---

[14] Although we refer to the Department's "policy" under section 607, it might be more accurate to characterize it as the Department's "practice." In either case, the legislative history of 28 U.S.C. § 592(c)(1)(B) suggests that an established practice of non-prosecution on given facts is within the scope of what the Attorney General must observe in determining whether to request appointment of an independent counsel. See Subcomm. on Oversight of Government Management of the Senate Comm. on Governmental Affairs, 97th Cong. 1st Sess., Report on Special Prosecutor Provisions of Ethics in Government Act of 1978 48 (Comm. Print 1981) ("The Subcommittee recognizes that there are instances in which a clear policy and clear Department of Justice precedent not to prosecute exist for a given violation, for all citizens.") (emphasis added); id. at 49 ("the Attorney General should be permitted to justify his decision that a special prosecutor should not be appointed upon a showing to the court that the Department of Justice does not, as a matter of established practice, prosecute the alleged violation of federal criminal law") (emphasis added); see also In re Nofziger, 925 F.2d at 449 (implying that a "prosecution practice" may constitute an established policy).

25

applied to the extensive use of Federal office space to mount a drive for political contributions, and we would not hesitate to use this statute as a prosecutive vehicle in an adequately aggravated situation of this sort.

Letter from Assistant Attorney General Patricia M. Wald, Office of Legislative Affairs, U.S. Department of Justice, to Senator Mark O. Hatfield, Feb. 24, 1978, at 7.

In 1978, the Department investigated allegations that President Carter had hosted a luncheon in the White House for about 20 prominent Democratic donors at which further contributions were solicited. Attorney General Griffin Bell declined to request the appointment of a special prosecutor because there was no evidence that anyone explicitly solicited or received money during the event. See Report of the Attorney General Pursuant to 28 U.S.C. § 592(b), Feb. 1, 1979, at 5, 9-10. Although the luncheon was intended to entertain former contributors in the hope that they would continue their financial support, the Attorney General concluded that such activity was not within the scope of former section 603, now renumbered 607. Id. at 10-11. The Report states:

> The Department of Justice is unaware of any instance in the ninety-six years since the statute was passed in which a prosecution was undertaken for the type of activity here at issue. * * *

> Moreover, when presented with factual situations involving isolated, non-egregious incidents of actual, explicit solicitations or receipts in federal buildings, the Department has consistently found them without prosecutive merit under Section 603. Thus, even assuming a much broader interpretation of the activity proscribed by Section 603, a prosecution of this matter would be legally unsound, unfair, and without merit.

26

Id. at 11-12.[15] The Attorney General's reference to the
Department's consistent practice of declining to prosecute
"isolated, non-egregious" violations of section 607 is another
way of stating the policy of declining to prosecute in the
absence of aggravating factors.

An additional valuable precedent also involves analysis
under the Independent Counsel Act of prosecutive policies under
section 607.[16] In 1988, two separate fundraising letters over
the signatures of two different Senators, both clearly addressed
to Department of Justice employees in their offices, were
delivered to the Department of Justice. At the time the letters
were received, an Attorney General Order extending the procedures
of the Independent Counsel Act to Members of Congress was in
effect. Attorney General Order No. 1297-88 (1988). In reviewing
this matter, the Election Crimes Branch of the Criminal Division

---

[15] This, of course, was before the provision was added to
the Independent Counsel Act directing Attorneys' General to take
Departmental policies into account in reaching decisions under
the Act. Thus, Attorney General Bell's final decision was based
on a lack of evidence that solicitations occurred, rather than on
the Department's prosecution policy. His articulation of
Department policy is consistent with every other articulation of
that policy found in the records.

[16] Unlike the preceding two articulations of the prosecution
policy, this document is not a public document, and the
Department of Justice does not ordinarily release such
declination memoranda. I have provided sufficient description of
the document to make its relevance here clear, and to demonstrate
the way in which the Departmental policy is repeatedly
articulated in the Departmental records concerning section 607.
In addition, I should make it clear here that these three
documents are offered simply as examples of previous
articulations of the Department's policy; there are many
additional non-public documents which reflect the policy.

recommended that to warrant prosecution, section 607 cases "normally require proof of some aggravating factor warranting the assessment of felony penalties, such as coercion or gross abuse of a federal workspace." Finding a "total absence here of any evidence of any intent to coerce involuntary political donations from federal personnel," the Branch recommended that the matter be closed. The Criminal Division in turn recommended, and the Attorney General agreed, that no independent counsel need be appointed to investigate the two Senators.

A number of different aggravating factors are mentioned in the Departmental records concerning section 607. They include, in addition to coercion, a demonstration of specific intent to flout the law, or conscious disregard of the law by one who has been put on notice of its requirements; a substantial number of violations; a substantial misuse of government resources or property in conjunction with the prohibited solicitations; and a substantial disruption of government functions resulting from the solicitations.

We have conducted, as is explained above, an extensive investigation of the Vice President's telephone solicitation calls, and I find no evidence in the investigative results that any of these aggravating factors is present. There is no evidence that the Vice President was specifically aware of the prohibitions of section 607, and no evidence that he was warned that his conduct would be in potential violation of that or any other statute. There are at most five telephone calls, even if

28

we draw every conceivable speculative inference against the Vice President, that could be construed as hard money solicitations, and hence potential violations of the law. The bulk of his calls were not charged to the government, and the few that were have been reimbursed. There is no suggestion that either the Vice President or any of the few staff members who were involved in these telephone solicitations neglected their official duties as a result.

Beyond these factors that have been specifically identified in Department of Justice records as potential aggravating circumstances in a section 607 case, I am unable to identify any other factors in this case that might properly be regarded as aggravating.

In short, the preliminary investigation has established that, even if the Vice President were found to have technically violated section 607, there is no evidence suggesting the presence of any aggravating factors of the sort that might warrant consideration of prosecution under established Departmental policy. Furthermore, I am unable to identify any way in which further investigation might lead to development of evidence of aggravating factors in this case. Therefore, in light of the clearly established policy of the Department of Justice that aggravating factors are required before prosecution of a section 607 matter can be considered, it is my obligation under the Independent Counsel Act to close this matter without seeking the appointment of an independent counsel.

29

CONCLUSION

The allegation that the Vice President may have been soliciting hard money is insubstantial, and depends so heavily on conjecture and speculation, that I conclude it does not provide reasonable grounds for further investigation. Indeed, I find clear and convincing evidence that the Vice President did not solicit hard money contributions in the course of his telephone conversations with prospective DNC donors. Furthermore, the established policy of the Department of Justice requires the presence of aggravating circumstances before a prosecution of a section 607 offense is warranted, and there is no evidence of any such circumstances here. Therefore, based on the results of the above-described investigation, I hereby notify this Court that no further investigation is warranted and no independent counsel need be appointed.

Respectfully submitted,

JANET RENO
Attorney General of the United States

DATE: December 7, 1997

United States Court of Appeals
For the District of Columbia Circuit

UNITED STATES COURT OF APPEALS FILED NOV 2 1998
FOR THE DISTRICT OF COLUMBIA CIRCUIT

Special Division

Division for the Purpose of
Appointing Independent Counsels

Ethics in Government Act of 1978, As Amended

In re: Albert Gore, Jr.

Before: SENTELLE, *Presiding Judge*, FAY and CUDAHY, *Senior Circuit Judges*

Order Authorizing Attorney General to Disclose
Notification of Results of Preliminary Investigation

Upon consideration of the request of the Attorney General pursuant to 28 U.S.C. § 592(c) for authorization to disclose the Notification to the Court Pursuant to U.S.C. § 592(b) of Results of Preliminary Investigation in this matter, which concerns matters that have been widely reported by the news media, it is hereby

ORDERED, in the public interest that leave is granted to the Attorney General pursuant to 28 U.S.C. § 592(e) to publicly disclose the Notification.

Per Curiam:
For the Court:

Mark J. Langer, Clerk

by

Marilyn R. Sargent
Chief Deputy Clerk

DOJ-02698

UNITED STATES COURT OF APPEALS
FOR THE DISTRICT OF COLUMBIA CIRCUIT
INDEPENDENT COUNSEL DIVISION

In re ALBERT GORE, JR.   )
)   No.
)

NOTIFICATION TO THE COURT PURSUANT TO 28 U.S.C. § 592(b)
OF RESULTS OF PRELIMINARY INVESTIGATION

On August 26, 1998, I notified this Court of the initiation
of a preliminary investigation of Vice President of the United
States Albert Gore, Jr. The preliminary investigation has now
been concluded, and I have determined that there are no
reasonable grounds to believe that further investigation is
warranted of the matters that were under investigation.
Therefore, appointment of an independent counsel is not being
sought. In accordance with the requirements of 28 U.S.C.
§ 592(b), this notification will summarize the information
received and the results of the preliminary investigation.

This preliminary investigation explored the question of
whether there is sufficient evidence to warrant further
investigation into whether the Vice President violated federal
law, 18 U.S.C. § 1001, when he told attorneys and investigators
last Fall that he did not know, at the time he made fundraising
telephone calls from his West Wing Office, that the beneficiary
of the solicitations, the media campaign run by the Democratic
National Committee (DNC), was funded in part with federal money,

-2-

and that he believed at the time of his telephone calls that
federal money contributions to the DNC were limited to $2,000.[1]

INFORMATION RECEIVED

a. The 1997 Investigation

In the Fall of 1997, the Department conducted a preliminary
investigation into the question of whether the Vice President may
have violated 18 U.S.C. § 607 when he made fundraising telephone
calls from his White House office (hereinafter, 1997
Investigation). The 1997 Investigation led to my conclusion that
there were no grounds to seek appointment of an independent
counsel for two independent reasons: first, the overwhelming
weight of the evidence supported the Vice President's statement
that he was soliciting soft money contributions, outside the
scope of section 607's ban on political fundraising from the
federal workplace, when he made the telephone calls, and second,
established Departmental policy precluded prosecutions under
section 607 in the absence of aggravating circumstances, such as
coercion, that were absent there.[2]

---

[1] Two additional allegations were received during the course
of the preliminary investigation that were related to the Vice
President's fundraising calls, but not to the specific matter
that was the subject of this preliminary investigation. An
initial inquiry was conducted into these allegations to determine
whether they were sufficiently specific and credible to warrant
further investigation into whether the Vice President may have
violated federal law. I have determined that they are not, and
they have been closed.

[2] These factual conclusions eliminated the necessity for me
to reach a determination as to whether section 607 applied to the
facts alleged.

-j-

In the course of the 1997 Investigation, we interviewed the Vice President. The Vice President explained that he believed he was soliciting soft money when he was making the telephone calls. The Vice President further explained that the telephone solicitations were intended to raise funds for the DNC's media fund, which financed a series of so-called "issue advertisements" that ran during late 1995 and 1996. He further explained that he believed at the time he made the calls that the DNC media campaign was financed entirely with soft money, and that donors were limited to $2000 in hard money contributions. This belief was erroneous,[1] but as a result, when he requested large contributions to the media fund, he believed that he could only have been requesting soft money contributions.[2] The Vice President understood that there was a hard money component to the DNC's overall budget, and that some of its activities had to be financed with hard money, but believed that because the media fund involved so-called "issue ads," it could be financed entirely with soft money.

---

[1] In fact, the advertisements were financed pursuant to a regulatory formula apportioning their cost between hard and soft money, and individual donors are permitted to contribute up to $20,000 to the DNC in hard money per calendar year, so long as their total hard money contributions to all donees do not exceed $25,000 per calendar year.

[2] As additional reasons why he intended to ask for soft money, the Vice President also pointed out that it was easier to raise soft money, especially corporate dollars, and that he believed that soft money is what the DNC needed at the time.

-4-

We explored this question further with the Vice President at the time, because we had obtained a number of memoranda addressed to the Vice President, among others, that mentioned the fact that the media campaign was funded with both hard and soft money, and we knew that a November 21, 1995 DNC budget meeting focused on the budget for the media fund. The agenda for the November 21 meeting suggested that the amount of funding for the media campaign and how to raise it was to have been a topic of discussion at the meeting, which we knew was attended by the Vice President.

The Vice President stated that he did not recall a discussion at this or any other meeting about the DNC's specific need for both hard and soft money in late 1995 to keep the advertisements on the air. The Vice President said that he believed that the fundraising phone calls probably were discussed during the meeting and that the general topic of the media fund budget being increased was raised and discussed. As for the memoranda that reflected a hard money component to the media fund, the Vice President said that as a rule he did not read memoranda on these topics, particularly from this author. This general practice was corroborated in the course of separate interviews with members of the Vice President's staff.

The Vice President's statements about his beliefs and intentions were a factor in my final conclusion in 1997 with respect to the alleged violations of 18 U.S.C. § 607, although a relatively minor one. Far more weighty was the substantial

-5-

evidence derived from interviews of the donors themselves which substantiated my conclusion that they were in fact solicited for large soft money contributions to the DNC, to support the DNC's media campaign.

b. The New Information

On July 27, 1998, long after the conclusion of the 1997 Investigation, the Vice President's counsel provided the Department with a six-page set of newly discovered documents, responsive to document requests we had made during the 1997 Investigation. The documents were a copy of a set of documents already in our possession, which were distributed at the November 1995 meeting referenced above. The copies provided by the Vice President's counsel, however, included handwritten notes by a member of the Vice President's staff that suggested that the hard money component to the media fund may have been expressly mentioned during the November 1995 meeting, which was attended by the Vice President.[3]

Specifically, the notes -- which set forth "65% soft/35% hard" opposite the term "media fund" -- appear to reflect a phrase that may have been used at the meeting to describe the approximate proportions of hard and soft money used by the DNC to purchase television ads during this period. The notes also include what may be a statement of the hard money limit for gifts

---

[3]While these newly discovered documents came from the Office of the Vice President, they did not come out of the Vice President's own files.

to the DNC. Specifically, the note just below the "65%/35%" includes what appears to be an attempt to explain that soft money contributions are "corporate or anything over $20 k from an individual." In addition, while not clearly written, a second notation that appears to say "hard limit $20k" appears on page two of the set of documents.

These new documents, then, raised some new questions concerning the Vice President's statements about his understanding of the DNC's efforts to fund the media campaign. The notes suggested that during the November 1995 meeting, both the fact that the hard money limit on donations to the DNC was $20,000, and that the media campaign was funded by a mix of hard and soft money may have been discussed in the Vice President's presence. This could give rise to an inference that his subsequent statements that he believed at the time that hard money donations to the DNC were limited to $2,000 and that the media campaign was funded only by soft money may have been false.

I therefore initiated a preliminary investigation of this matter to fully explore the evidence concerning the Vice President's knowledge and intent.

APPLICABLE LAW

The false statement statute provides, in pertinent part:

> [w]hoever, in any matter within the jurisdiction of the executive, legislative, or judicial branch of the Government of the United States, knowingly and willfully . . . makes any materially false, fictitious, or fraudulent statement or representation shall be [guilty of a felony].

-7-

18 U.S.C. § 1001. To obtain a conviction under section 1001, the government must prove (1) a statement, (2) falsity, (3) materiality, (4) specific intent, and (5) agency jurisdiction. United States v. Herring, 916 F.2d 1543, 1546 (11th Cir.1990), cert. denied, 500 U.S. 946 (1991). The elements in issue here are falsity and criminal intent; the other elements of the offense are not in dispute.

SCOPE OF THE INVESTIGATION

The handwritten notes alone are not sufficient to warrant a conclusion that the Vice President made a false statement. In an effort to determine whether the apparent disparity between what the Vice President told us he believed at the time he made the calls and what the notes indicate may have been said at a meeting he attended on these topics warrants further investigation, we interviewed the attendees of the meeting and others involved with these topics. These witnesses included the Vice President, current and former members of his staff, other current and former White House officials, officials of the Clinton/Gore `96 Committee (Clinton/Gore `96), and various officers and employees of the DNC. Documents were also obtained from the White House, the DNC, Clinton/Gore `96, and others, including an affidavit from the Vice President's counsel. We also reviewed depositions and testimony provided by various witnesses in the course of previous congressional and task force inquiries into various campaign fundraising matters. Finally, we reviewed all other

-8-

documents and evidence that might support an inference that the Vice President's statements were false.

We were seeking to determine whether there was any evidence from which one might reasonably infer that the Vice President actually knew about the hard money component of the media campaign or the $20,000 contribution limit at the time he made the telephone calls seeking contributions. Such an inference might be supported, for example, by information that these facts were discussed in sufficient detail and focus at the meeting that many other attendees specifically recall them, that the Vice President made comments or asked questions in the course of the discussion that would seem to reflect an active understanding of the details, that the participants recall any affirmative discussion of a need to raise hard money for the media fund, that the Vice President read memoranda that made these points, or that anyone spoke directly to the Vice President on any occasion about the need to raise hard money for the media campaign.

RESULTS OF THE INVESTIGATION

As a threshold matter, the evidence we gathered during these interviews does support a conclusion that the Vice President attended a DNC budget meeting on November 21, 1995, and that at some point in the course of the meeting, the DNC media fund was discussed. The evidence also supports a conclusion that some reference was made in the course of the meeting to the fact that there was a hard money component to the financing of the media campaign.

Fifteen individuals, including the President and Vice President, attended the meeting. All fifteen were interviewed, with two exceptions: one who testified under oath in the course of a congressional investigation that he had no recollection of the meeting, and that if he attended at all, he likely would have left after just a few minutes; and the President, who provided us with a statement that he had no independent recollection of the meeting.

No attendees recall any particular questions or comments by the Vice President. No one who arrived at the meeting without a working knowledge of the DNC financing issues left with an accurate understanding of the fact that both hard and soft money were necessary to pay for the media campaign. Only two of the fifteen attendees at the meeting even recall the topic of a hard money component to the media fund being raised during the meeting.

While the author of the notes had no specific recollection of the meeting, he did confirm, based on his habit and practice, his belief that the words noted in his handwriting were things said during the meeting that he recorded as they were said. Reviewing his notes, this attendee could not recall who might have uttered the words "65% soft/35% hard"; "corporate or anything over $20k from an individual"; or "hard money limit $20k" during the meeting. He was also unable to provide an explanation about what each of the phrases might have meant within the context of the meeting. He did not recall the issue

of "hard" and "soft" money being discussed by those attending but
noted that these issues were often discussed at DNC budget
meetings. He was also unable to say whether the words were used
with regard to the media fund, the DNC's operating budget, or
something else. Notably, this individual, who attended the
meeting and was paying enough attention to what was being said to
take verbatim notes of some points, also told us during his
interview that he believed that the media campaign was financed
entirely with soft money.

Two attendees specifically recall references to hard money
in connection with the media fund being made at the meeting. The
first, a White House official, recalls that the hard money
component to the media fund was discussed. He also recalls a
discussion of how much would have to be raised both in hard and
in soft dollars for the media fund during the meeting. However,
he has no specific recollection of any of the statements recorded
in the notes.[6]

The other, a DNC official, was the individual who made one
of the quoted statements. He recalls answering a question about
the "spending side" of the media campaign by noting that the
expenses were generally averaging "65% soft/35% hard".[7] The
answer, according to this attendee, was one sentence without any

---

[6] He also said that while he does not recall a specific
conversation about the limit on hard money contributions to the
DNC, it would not surprise him if it was discussed.

[7] This phrase mirrors the handwritten note made on the
first page of the packet.

elaboration. He does not remember who asked the question but
volunteered that he did not think it was the Vice President since
the Vice President did not often get into "that level of detail".
He had no memory of anyone else mentioning hard or federal money
during this preliminary discussion of the "spending side" of the
media campaign. He does not recall a specific use of the terms
hard, soft, federal or non-federal money during the discussion
that centered around the "spending side" of the DNC.

He did remember some discussion about the fact that the DNC
had sufficient funds available to borrow on their hard money line
of credit but no borrowing capacity on the soft money side.
There was a discussion about direct mail contributions to the DNC
operating budget -- all in hard money -- that were available, if
needed, for the media purchases. He recalled that both of these
facts were mentioned as reasons why there was sufficient hard
money on hand to keep the advertisements on the air through the
end of the year, but that soft money would need to be raised.[8]
According to this witness, after these points were made at the
meeting, the ensuing conversation about the funding of the media
campaign and the money needed to be raised by the President and
Vice President would have been focused on the need for soft
money.

---

[8] He could not say who addressed these topics or how long
the discussion lasted but, instead, characterized it as a
"general discussion" involving more than one person.

-12-

As noted above, in order to prove a violation of Section 1001 in this case, the government would have to prove beyond a reasonable doubt that, at the time he made the telephone calls that were at issue in the 1997 Investigation, the Vice President actually knew that the media campaign had a hard money component, or that the limit on hard money contributions was $20,000. In this case, there is no direct evidence of such knowledge. While the Vice President was present at the meeting, there is no evidence that he heard the statements or understood their implications, so as to suggest the falsity of his statement two years later that he believed the media fund was entirely soft money. Nor does anyone recall the Vice President asking any questions or making any comments at the meeting about the media fund, much less questions or comments indicating an understanding of the issue of the blend of hard and soft money needed for DNC media expenditures. Witnesses were also asked whether they recalled any other discussion with the Vice President about the hard money component of the media fund; none recalled any, nor did any recall the Vice President saying or doing anything at any other time that would indicate that indeed he knew, whether from the meeting or from some other source, that there was a hard money component to the media fund.

There is thus only weak circumstantial evidence of the Vice President's knowledge -- his presence at a meeting where the subject was briefly discussed -- which I do not believe provides reasonable grounds to believe that further investigation of this

-13-

matter is warranted. Notably, others attending the meeting also left it with an inaccurate understanding of the funding of the media campaign. The range of impressions and vague misunderstandings among all the meeting attendees is striking, and undercuts any reasonable inference that mere attendance at the meeting should have served to communicate to the Vice President an accurate understanding of the facts.

In addition to the total lack of direct evidence suggesting that the Vice President was aware of the hard money component to the media fund, and the insubstantial nature of even the indirect evidence, I also find a lack of evidence to reasonably support a conclusion that he may have had a motive to falsely deny that he knew about the hard money component. The documentary evidence and the testimony from involved witnesses clearly establish that at the time, the DNC did not need to find ways of raising hard money in order to continue to run the advertisements. However, it was critically short of soft money, and had used up its soft money line of credit. Thus, when the Vice President was asked to help raise money by making telephone solicitations, the DNC's specific need was for soft money.

In other words, the Vice President did not need to deny knowledge of the fact that there was a hard money component to the fund in order to provide an innocent explanation for his telephone calls. His explanation would have been just as innocent if he had stated that while he knew there was a hard money component to the media campaign, soft money was what was needed at the time and therefore that was what he was raising. In fact, such an account, unlike the one he gave, would have been corroborated by the documentary evidence that was brought to the Vice President's attention.

It is also significant that there is evidence that this issue was specifically brought to the Vice President's attention before his interview with us during the 1997 Investigation. The Vice President's attorneys have provided us with their sworn statement that in the course of preparing him for his interview, the Vice President also told them that at the time he made the calls he believed that the media campaign was funded entirely with soft money. They explained to him that this belief was not accurate, and pointed out to him that there were documents, addressed to him, in conflict with his statement. Nevertheless, they averred, he stated that he would have to tell us that he believed the media fund was all soft money because it was the truth.

To summarize, it appears that at the time of his interview during the 1997 Investigation, the Vice President was expressly aware that he had little to gain and much to lose in admitting his misconception of the true facts. In fact, his explanation not only led to additional inquiries during the 1997 Investigation, because it was at odds with known documents, but led directly to this investigation as well. I can see no reasonable basis for concluding that he had a motive to tell this story if it were not true.

-15-

As mentioned above, the Vice President also told us in the course of the 1997 Investigation that he believed that the limit on hard money contributions was $2000, and some of the handwritten notes suggest that topic too may have been discussed at the November 1995 meeting. However, while some of the fifteen meeting attendees had a vague recollection of some of the topics of discussion, no one interviewed could remember the use of the note's terms "hard limit $20 k" and "corporate or anything over $20k from an individual" in this meeting. We thus have no evidence of what, if anything, was said, or in what context. Thus, with the exception of the notes themselves, the meaning of which is unclear, we are left with no evidence that the Vice President's statement that he believed the legal limit for hard money gifts to the DNC was the same as the limit for individual candidates -- $2,000 per election cycle -- is false. We found no independent evidence to suggest that the Vice President did not in fact believe that hard money contributions were so limited, and his belief is plausible in light of his previous experience with congressional campaigns.[9] While it appears from the handwritten notes that some reference to the higher limit on hard money contributions to the DNC may have been made during the meeting, the fact that no one who attended the meeting recalled the statement — and a number of other attendees reported the same or similar mistaken belief about the limitation on the size

---

[9] The limit for contributions to an individual candidate is $1,000 or, in the case of a married couple, $2,000.

of hard money contributions — leads me to the conclusion that I
have insufficient evidence to warrant further investigation as to
whether the Vice President made a false statement on this point.

As mentioned above, in the course of the 1997 Investigation,
we obtained several memoranda addressed to the Vice President as
one of several recipients, which contain brief internal
references to the hard money component to the media fund.
However, as we noted at the conclusion of the 1997 Investigation,
the Vice President has stated, and several members of his staff
have confirmed, that he did not read these types of memoranda
that dealt with DNC budgetary issues. We discovered no new
evidence during this investigation which contradicts this
evidence or would lead me to revisit my previous conclusion that
the mere existence of these memoranda, without any evidence that
the Vice President actually read them, was not sufficient grounds
to conclude that the Vice President might have been making a
false statement about his knowledge of the hard money component
to the media fund.

Finally, there were regular meetings held at the White House
known as "Residence Meetings," because they were held in the
White House. During the relevant period, the Residence Meetings
were focused on political strategy and polling issues. Two
Residence Meeting "agendas" -- one dated September 7, 1995 and
the other dated September 13, 1995 -- have one line each that
indicates that the DNC issue ads under consideration were going
to be paid for, in part, with hard money.

We were unable to establish whether the Vice President attended these particular meetings; indeed, we have been unable to establish that those two meetings were even held. They do not appear on either the President's or the Vice President's daily calendars, while other Residence Meetings do appear. Regular attendees of the Residence Meetings who were interviewed do not recall whether these particular meetings were held, or if they were held, whether the Vice President attended or whether these particular agenda items were actually discussed. Many of the attendees specifically stated that they do not recall the hard money component to the media fund ever being discussed at the Residence Meetings.[10] Given this state of the evidence, I conclude that there is insufficient evidence to reasonably conclude that the Vice President was put on notice as to the hard

---

[10]One attendee, in the course of a single interview, first stated that he was unaware that there was a hard money component to the media fund and that he had no idea there was hard money in the DNC. He believed any "hard money" advertising was paid for by Clinton/Gore '96. He stated he had no idea whether the Vice President knew there was a hard money component to the DNC media campaign. Later in the same interview, after being advised of the contents of the agendas for the September 7 and 13 meetings, he said he had been mistaken; that he did know all along that there was a hard money component, that it was discussed during the Residence meetings, and that he believed the Vice President also knew, though he had no specific knowledge on which he based that belief. He thought it was "likely" that the Vice President attended the September 7 and 13 meetings.

Given the inconsistencies within this witness's statements, the lack of any specific knowledge upon which he bases his stated beliefs about the Vice President's presence or knowledge, and the contradictory statements of other regular attendees at the Residence meetings, I do not find the statement of this one witness persuasive enough to warrant further investigation.

money component to the media fund during or because of any
discussion that may have been held on the topic in the course of
the Residence Meetings.

I considered with care the reasonable implications that
might be drawn from all of this evidence -- the Vice President's
attendance at the November 1995 meeting, the memoranda addressed
to him, and the Residence meetings -- along with all other
evidence and information available to us concerning the Vice
President's understanding of the media fund and how it was
financed, including the affidavit of the Vice President's
counsel. Taken altogether, I find the evidence fails to provide
any reasonable support for a conclusion that the Vice President
may have lied. As explained above, there are no reasonable
grounds to conclude that the November 1995 meeting would have put
the Vice President on notice of the hard money component of the
media fund, there is no evidence that the Vice President actually
read the memoranda in which the topic is mentioned (and
considerable evidence that he did not), and there is insufficient
evidence that the topic was addressed at the Residence Meetings
or that the Vice President attended the meetings where the topic
might have been raised. As a result, I conclude that there is no
reasonable prospect that these facts could support a successful
prosecution. Furthermore, I am unable to identify any additional

investigation that might reasonably be expected to provide
sufficient evidence to support a successful prosecution.[11]

CONCLUSION

I conclude that the evidence supporting a conclusion that
the Vice President may have provided false statements to
investigators and attorneys during an interview in the 1997
Investigation is so insubstantial that there are no reasonable
grounds for further investigation. Therefore, based on the
results of the above-described investigation, I hereby notify
this Court that no independent counsel should be appointed.

Respectfully submitted,

JANET RENO
Attorney General of the United States

DATE: _November 24, 1998_

---

[11] "If the "clear and convincing evidence" standard were
applicable to this determination, I would find by clear and
convincing evidence that the Vice President did not lie.

Senator KYL. Since no one, and I want to make this clear, there is a bit of a straw man here about your independence, I know of no one who has ever questioned whether you are independent enough. The question, I think, is whether you are too independent or too independent at least of the advice of some very top professionals who were brought in to give you advice.

Now, we know who did recommend appointment of special counsel; people like Charles La Bella, and Mr. Conrad, Mr. Freeh. My question is this: Were there others? And I presume that some of the staff people of these people also recommended that. And to have rejected their advice, it seems to me, you must really have had confidence in the advice of the others who came to a different conclusion. Could you tell us who those people are.

Attorney General RENO. I cannot give you each person who I sought advice from with respect to each matter, but I will try to make sure that you have as much as I can pull together. I think you have all of the documents, and I think that is where I rely primarily.

The CHAIRMAN. Senator Kyl, we have stopped others at this point.

Senator KYL. Yes, and I am happy to be stopped. I presume, then, you will submit for the record the names of the people that you relied upon in addition.

Attorney General RENO. Senator, I am trying to tell you that I think we have given the committee all of the information with respect to what was in writing. I do not know that I can go back and give you everybody that I have relied on. But as I told you, I will try to do my best.

Senator KYL. I would appreciate that. Thank you.

The CHAIRMAN. We will have a second round, Senator Kyl.

Senator Feinstein.

Senator FEINSTEIN. Thanks very much, Mr. Chairman.

Madam Attorney General, I have been privileged to be on this committee during your entire tenure, and I can certainly say no one has been more resistant to political pressure, tougher or more independent than you. And I think you have made that very clear. I think when Senator Torricelli mentioned that you have essentially triggered an independent counsel for five of your fellow colleagues on the Cabinet, plus the President of the United States himself, I think that is a pretty good testament to independence.

As I read the regulations that govern the appointment of special counsel, the decision of whether to appoint a special counsel is vested in you, the Attorney General, not those who advise you, unless you recuse yourself from the issue. The decision is not in the hands of the director of the FBI or the head of the Campaign Financing Task Force or any other person, other than you.

Would you tell me if I am correct in understanding the law. And can you explain the corrosive impact on the authority of the Attorney General, any Attorney General, of subordinates publicly leaking the recommendations that are entrusted, by law, to the discretion of the Attorney General, himself or herself.

Attorney General RENO. I think you are correct in the law. And I think leaks are very damaging to good, fruitful conversation. But my policy has been I do not walk away from it. I just try to let people know how damaging leaks can be. But I still try to reach out to a variety of people, those that say yes and those that say no, because I find that sometimes they change their positions and sometimes they are advocating another point of view.

I think this Nation, as I said at the outset, the foundation of this Nation is spirited debate, and I think it is important that we have it.

Senator FEINSTEIN. But the point I wanted to establish is you could essentially have everyone advising you to do one thing, and you could turn around, within your discretion, and do exactly the opposite. But when somebody that works in this confidential capacity essentially leaks the advice they give you, it effectively corrodes the authority of the institution of Attorney General itself, and I think sets a kind of precedent, which does not brook well for this particular office, which after all is one of the chief law enforcement officer for the Nation, where staff serving that officer should be able to do so in confidence and certainly without leaking.

Attorney General RENO. I would agree with you, but I am not going to let it corrode it.

Senator FEINSTEIN. Well, I hope not, and I appreciate that very much.

Thanks, Mr. Chairman.

The CHAIRMAN. Thank you very much, Senator Feinstein.

Senator Sessions.

Senator SESSIONS. Thank you, Mr. Chairman.

I think, Attorney General Reno, that maybe we are, at times, too hard on a team of prosecutors struggling with difficult issues. But we are dealing with an unusual case, a case of national importance, that has been followed since the story broke late in the 1996 election cycle and needs to be brought to rest with thorough investigation and thorough knowledge.

So I think we should be reluctant to impose ourselves on the Department of Justice. But when a string of lawyers and people chosen by you, such as Mr. Litt, Mr. La Bella and now Mr. Conrad, all say that an independent counsel ought to be appointed, I think that requires us to give it most serious consideration, and the public is entitled to this exchange, so that you have to talk about it, and we can perhaps ask some questions about it.

One of the things that I think is important to note is the circumstances involving the Buddhist Temple fundraiser. To me, from the beginning of the fundraising issues, this one struck me as the one that could be most troublesome to the Vice President and others. There has been a concern about the phone calls, and perhaps that may or may not be a violation, may not be a violation that would be worthy of a prosecution, but there were some serious issues raised.

We know that it was indeed a political fundraiser, and Maria Hsia has been convicted of felonies related to that event. We know it is a criminal violation to file false campaign contribution reports. It is a criminal violation to make a political fundraiser appear to be a nonpolitical event in order to circumvent income tax laws that prohibit taxexempt organizations from doing fundraisers. It is a criminal violation to conspire with others to commit any of those crimes under title 18, section 371, and it is a violation of 1001, the False Statements Act, to make a false statement to investigators.

So that is a matter of real seriousness to me, and this is a matter apparently Mr. Conrad has just now become focused on. He has been in office about 6 months, I understand, and for the first time in 4 years, the Vice President has now been interviewed about this event. And last Thursday, after that interview, we learned that Mr. Conrad has now recommended a special counsel to investigate possible criminal violations by the Vice President.

Last Friday afternoon, the Vice President has released a transcript showing his answers to the questions. However, the public does not know and probably shouldn't know all the information that was available to Mr. Conrad, your chosen prosecutor, when he decided it was appropriate to do a special counsel.

So I am concerned about that, and I was impressed with Mr. Conrad because he seemed to me to be a line prosecutor of solid experience. And I believe that he had the kind of background that probably would lead him to make good decisions in this case. He certainly did not appear to be a person that was grandstanding in any way.

Now, the transcript shows that the focus of the investigation was on the people who were there at that fundraiser and their relationship with the Vice President. And I think that is important.

Also, I would want to suggest that in the prosecutions I have done in 15 years with the Department of Justice, I have been involved in cases which I personally prosecuted county commissioners, mayors, judges, sheriffs, chiefs of police, and those kinds of cases. Normally the question comes down to a question of knowledge. We can prove that an illegal fundraiser occurred. We can prove that foreign money was placed into the Democratic National Committee coffers. We can prove that money was laundered through the nuns, conduit violations of the law. The question simply is: Does the Vice President know? Is he knowledgeable about these things that went on all around him?

That is the question. And it is easy for someone to say I didn't know, but a good investigator and a good prosecutor, in my opinion, in my experience, has to be prepared to go further and to look at other evidence.

Now, I hope and pray that there is nothing here that would implicate the Vice President seriously in these matters. However, I think there is some evidence that raises questions.

Earlier it was suggested that the Vice President's schedule was not clear about whether or not it was fundraiser, but his schedule, which I have a copy of, said DNC luncheon at Hacienda Heights—that is the area in question—$1,000, $5,000 per head, 150 to 200 people. That indicates to me in pretty common language that it was a fundraiser. And he has denied that. The Vice President has flatly denied that he knew it was a fundraiser.

We also have an e-mail that he personally sent after being inquired by e-mail whether he would want to go to New York because to do so would conflict with two fundraisers—"two fundraisers in San Jose and L.A." And he was told we have confirmed the fundraisers for Monday, April 29, the day of this temple fundraiser. Vice President Gore responded: If we book the two fundraisers, we have to decline—that is, decline the New York invitation. That would indicate that he had information that this would be a fundraiser. So we are looking at some very, very serious matters, in my opinion.

My time has run out. I would be delighted——

Attorney General RENO. I would agree that Robert Conrad is a fine prosecutor, an ethical man, and very diligent, and I have a great admiration for him.

Senator SPECTER. Senator Feingold.

Senator FEINGOLD. Thank you, Mr. Chairman.

Madam Attorney General, welcome. I also want to join with others in saying I have enjoyed working with you over the years on a wide variety of matters, and I appreciate the dedication and professionalism of the Department of Justice.

I will use my limited time to make a few brief comments, and, of course, if you wish to respond, please do so.

One area where we have differed, Madam Attorney General, is in our approach to the enforcement of the campaign finance laws. As you know, I first called for an independent counsel to investigate campaign finance violations in the 1996 elections over 3 years ago. I was one of only two Democratic Senators to do so. I believed then and I believe now that there were serious abuses of the law by both political parties in the 1996 campaign, and that an independent investigation is the only way to get to the bottom of the abuses in a way that will command public confidence.

Let me stress, as this political season is upon us, that I said that both parties' fundraising activities should be scrutinized in such an investigation, and, Madam Attorney General, congressional elections should be a part of it.

Those who call for a partisan investigation or to limit it to certain events seem generally to seek an investigation to accomplish political goals rather than to uncover all of the abuses of our current laws that have occurred.

I also believe that some of the same activities of questionable legality that arose in the 1996 campaign are going on today. In particular, both Presidential campaigns are taking advantage of loopholes in the campaign finance law by participating in television advertising campaigns funded with soft money donations. These ads, which have already hit the airwaves, are billed as "party-building" issue ads. They talk about the candidates. They show their faces. They promote them and attack their opponents. But they avoid the use of the so-called magic words of express advocacy that would make them clearly illegal.

Madam Attorney General, I have never accepted the flawed legal opinion under which both parties and their candidates are now operating and its perverse conclusion that the "magic words" distinction applies to ads run by the parties. We all know that if a candidate runs an ad, it must be paid for with hard money whether or not it uses the magic words. I think the same should apply to parties who run ads supporting their candidates or attacking another party's candidate.

Nothing in the *Buckley* case suggests that parties should be treated more like independent groups than like candidate with respect to this issue. The participation of the two major Presidential campaigns in the use of the soft money loophole to fund phony issue ads is unseemly and wrong. Once nominated, each of the major Presidential candidates will receive over $65 million in public funds to run his general election campaign. The taxpayers of this country have a right to expect them to abide by the spirit as well as the letter of the law if they are going to take advantage of this public financing system.

I understand that outside watchdogs, Common Cause and Democracy 21, have indicated that they intend to request a Department of Justice investigation of the ongoing Presidential campaigns, and I think it would be entirely appropriate for you to conduct such investigation or, Madam Attorney General, to appoint a special counsel to do so.

As I have said over and over again, however, any such investigation should include both parties and both Presidential and congressional campaigns. This problem is not unique to one party or to the Presidential race.

Madam Attorney General, I appreciate the dilemma you are in. I think it is entirely appropriate for you to attempt to keep the Department's criminal investigations out of politics. Unfortunately, the very nature of these allegations make that very difficult. And so I make this recommendation: Madam Attorney General, appoint a special counsel with a wide-ranging mandate to investigate campaign finance violations in both the 1996 and 2000 campaign; insist that the special counsel consider allegations of wrongdoing by both parties and in both the Presidential and congressional campaigns; remove this issue to some extent from partisan debate by authorizing an investigation that is deliberate, complete, and detailed.

I understand that this investigation may not be completed by November, but it will put the parties and the candidates on notice that their activities in this upcoming election will be closely scrutinized. And if that leads the parties and the campaigns to be less aggressive in exploiting loopholes in current law that the Congress has thus far failed to close, that will be a beneficial side effect of your decision.

Thank you, Mr. Chairman, and I appreciate the opportunity to make a statement.

Senator SPECTER. Do you care to comment, Attorney General Reno?

Attorney General RENO. I remember in April of 1997 your thoughtful comments. They were constructive, and I have remembered them for a long time, and I appreciate them.

I don't pass judgment on the Federal Election Campaign Act or its effectiveness in making my determinations. What I have got to do is be able, if I am going to prosecute, to show that the conduct is willful, that the violation is willful and knowing.

I have conducted an extensive investigation on the issue. The advice of counsel defense is there. It won't go away. Under the Independent Counsel Act, I made the determination that further investigation would produce nothing. I think the answers have got to be found in another arena to address the issues that you are talking about, but I would look forward to working with you.

Senator FEINGOLD. Thank you very much.

Senator SPECTER. Senator Smith.

Senator SMITH. Thank you, Mr. Chairman.

Madam Attorney General, I am just trying to understand how you arrived at your judgment. I respect the fact that you have the right to make this judgment over the recommendations of people who work for you, which you have described as competent, intelligent, dedicated people. But without replaying the whole thing, I mean, you have—in November of 1997, you have Freeh saying I am convinced now more than ever this should be referred to an independent counsel; La Bella again saying he recommended the appointment, and that is in July 1998; in November of 1998, Litt saying, "One could infer that Gore knew what he claimed he did not know, that the media campaign was paid for in part with hard money"; and now the latest with Mr. Conrad, and then on top of that you have the Vice President in his deposition before Mr. Conrad saying, "I sure as hell did not have any conversations with anyone saying this is a fundraising event." That is what he told the investigators. Senator Sessions just showed the memo which referred to so much per head.

I have been to fundraisers many times, as we all have. I went to one this morning. I knew what I was going to, and I knew how much the price was for the person that I attended for.

So my only question to you is, they work for you, you make the call, and you did. But don't you think the public has a right to know what went through your mind in making that call. Why did you overrule those four people and at the same time ignore information that was out there in the domain about Mr. Gore?

And I would add one other thing. Maria Hsia was a longtime associate of Vice President Gore, of Senator Gore, and he had known her back at least as far as 1989, and she had done fundraising for him. And he was aware that Maria Hsia was at this event and had a lot to do with coordinating the event. And I just have one follow-on question, if you could just respond to that. I am just interested in how do you make this judgment. How do you make that judgment? What did you—what went through your mind to overrule those four people and the other information?

Attorney General RENO. First of all, you give the impression that I overrule all my advisers.

Senator SMITH. No. I just said these four.

Attorney General RENO. Well, the reason I made my determination is expressed in notifications filed with the court that had been a matter of public record, and I will be happy to make those available to you, Senator. They have been made available and are publicly available.

With respect to the prosecutions and what we have done, there have been approximately 25 prosecutions and 20 convictions.

With respect to the present matter, as I said at the outset, I am not going to comment on pending investigations. I think it is imperative for justice to be done that people don't comment until they have all the facts. That includes me. I am going to conduct a thorough review of everything. I am going to make my best judgment. But I would urge you with all my heart, be careful as you comment that you have the facts.

Senator SMITH. Well, so you are saying that it is still ongoing. In your mind, you are still looking into this matter. Is that correct?

Attorney General RENO. I am not commenting on what I am doing, but I think it imperative for justice to be done that an investigation be conducted without public discussion so that it could be done the right way.

Senator SMITH. Well, it started in November of 1997, as far as we know, with Mr. Freeh's memo, so it is 3 years later. I don't know when we get it done. Sometime, I guess, by the end of this century, maybe.

The final question that I have, I don't understand for the life of me why any individual would deny that he or she attended a fundraiser. Attending a fundraiser is not a bad thing. Now, it was an embarrassing fundraiser in the sense that nuns were asked to contribute money. I will grant you that. But why would any individual say I didn't attend—I don't know, excuse me, that it was a fundraiser when all this documentation proves otherwise. So I think it would go to the next question. Foreign contributions were passed at that fundraiser. So if you are going to continue your investigation, I would hope that somebody might ask the Vice President a little bit about how much he knew about whether or not there were foreign contributions. He was asked that in the Conrad questioning, and he said that, of course not, I did not know that illegal contributions of foreign contributions had been solicited.

But it makes no sense to me that somebody would deny they are attending a fundraiser when, in fact, everybody knows they attended a fundraiser. His schedule says he attended a fundraiser. And his background briefing papers say he attended a fundraiser, and the dollars that are going to be at that fundraiser are indicated. So there is something here that we don't know about that makes no sense to me, and that is where I am at.

I mean, attending a fundraiser is not bad. We all do it. But attending a fundraiser with illegal contributions is bad if you know it. And my concern is that we don't have the answer to that question.

Attorney General RENO. I cannot comment on a pending investigation, but I can——

Senator SMITH. Well, obviously you are not going to but——

Attorney General RENO. But I can comment on the need for everyone to let an investigation be conducted the right way. As you point out, you don't know something. Let's wait until we do it the right way and find out as much information as possible.

Senator SMITH. Should the American people know this before the election?

Senator SPECTER. Senator Smith, we have stopped everybody at this point.

Senator SMITH. Fine.

Senator SPECTER. We will have another round.

Senator Schumer.

Senator SCHUMER. Thank you, Mr. Chairman.

Mr. Chairman, to the extent that we are today examining whether the Attorney General should appoint a special counsel to investigate the 1996 election, I feel compelled to say that the committee is acting beyond its purview and, therefore, risks being labeled as partisan. Our role in these matter is one of oversight. I am worried, however, that if we are here quizzing the Attorney General on a decision she has not yet made, this committee will be perceived as going beyond oversight and instead attempting to influence an executive branch decision that should be made on the merits and on the merits alone.

This is ironic because the Justice Department is being criticized here for making decisions based on political influence and not on the merits. Yet this committee now appears to be applying a pressure of its own.

I have no questions.

Senator SPECTER. Thank you very much, Senator Schumer.

Attorney General Reno, would you care to take a break?

Attorney General RENO. I am fine. Thank you, sir.

Senator SPECTER. The second round will also be 5 minutes. In very brief response to what Senator Schumer has had to say, the questions have related to the decisions made by Attorney General Reno in declining independent counsel as to the Vice President, the decision already made, declining independent counsel as to the President and Vice President. Her appearance was requested on May 25, which was substantially in advance of the information as to Mr. Conrad's recommendation.

Attorney General Reno, I am going to come back and——

Senator SCHUMER. Mr. Chairman, if I might just respond?

Senator SPECTER. All right. We will stop the clock. Go ahead, Senator Schumer. You had some time left.

Senator SCHUMER. Once it is known there is an ongoing investigation into these matters, there shouldn't have been a hearing.

Senator SPECTER. Well, I disagree with that. But this is the first time that it has been raised, and had you raised it earlier, I would have been willing to consider it. You and I have talked about the matters, and I would always give consideration to whatever you had to say. This is the first time I have heard your comment.

Attorney General Reno, I am going to go into some detail, as soon as I have the time to do so, about the number of witnesses who had testimony that the Vice President knew about hard money and also about the advice of counsel defense which you have talked about, and also the issue of pressure which has been raised. But I want to talk for a moment and ask you about a broader question, and the broader question that I want to broach is the lateness of the Department of Justice's inquiry.

You and I first started to talk about this matter in April 1997, more than 3 years ago, and in November of 1997, FBI Director Freeh called for independent counsel. And within a week a letter was addressed to you by me asking for his report so we could get to the specifics.

And on July 16, 1998, La Bella submitted a memorandum calling for independent counsel, and on the 23rd of July, I had asked for that report.

Now, we have had the recommendation of Mr. Litt, one of your top deputies, calling for independent counsel. And it was not until April 18th of this year, just 2 months ago, that the Vice President was questioned about the Hsi Lai Buddhist Temple and about the coffees, although those matters were well known back in 1997 and were commented on extensively by the Governmental Affairs Committee at that time. And it appears that the questioning of the Vice

President on April 18 may have been motivated by the fact that the Judiciary Committee finally—finally—issued subpoenas for the Freeh and La Bella memoranda which were returnable on April 20. And they were known to the Justice Department several weeks in advance of that time, so that the Justice Department finally got around to asking the Vice President about the Hsi Lai Temple and the coffees on April 18th, although the Vice President had been questioned on four prior occasions.

Now, it appears to me that it may well be too late at this point to have special counsel—that is the name now under the Attorney General's regulationsbecause it would interfere with the election in 2000. And it is curious that matters arising out of the 1996 election should not have been laid to rest long ago when they were the focus of attention within a few months after the 1996 election.

I would be interested in your comments, although I am pretty sure of the answer, as to whether special counsel could be appointed and clear the Vice President before the Democratic Convention. And I think that is not realistic, probably not even realistic to have special counsel appointed and clear the Vice President or not clear the Vice President before the general election.

Now, it may be that the only alternative America has at this point in this election is to leave it to the political process with the Vice President stating his position and his opponent in a Presidential campaign stating his position. And it may be only 20/20 hindsight, but in light of the very emphatic statements you made when you came for confirmation, asking this committee to approve you, which we did, asking for our votes, which I cast in the affirmative, about the need to have somebody outside to give credibility, no matter how professional and credible the Attorney General is. And I have never questioned your credibility or your integrity. But you said that the only way to do it—you quoted Archibald Cox—was to have somebody from the outside.

Now, a focus of the question is: Why so late? It is true you made the decisions before. A two-part question: As close as the matter was with your own view of independence and with the body of evidence available, why not then? And why now? Why ask a new chief counsel of your campaign task force to question the Vice President on April 18th when it is too late because the matter can't be resolved in a timely way for this election?

Attorney General RENO. I can't comment with respect to the specifics, but I can talk to you generally about how an investigation is conducted. That is like preaching to the choir because you are an experienced prosecutor. And in some—

Senator SPECTER. Madam Attorney General, may I interrupt you? This is the first time and the last time I will do it, I think.

The Vice President has disclosed publicly that he was questioned on April 18, and Mr. Conrad confirmed that. So it is not a disclosure. We know that happened. Why was he questioned on April 18th? What can be accomplished at this late date?

Attorney General RENO. First of all, you alluded to the release of the La Bella and Freeh memoranda. Let me point out to you that both Director Freeh and Mr. La Bella have consistently been opposed to the release of it because at the time they were concerned that it would give a road map to the course of the investigation and would be counterproductive to the investigation.

For me to discuss why something was done when would do the same thing, and it is not right to discuss it.

What I can talk about in generalities and not reference a specific case, you probably didn't have prosecutors in your office, but I sometimes had prosecutors in my office that would go interview somebody without having all the facts. And the interview was not nearly as good as the prosecutor who went armed with all the facts, working towards the issues. And I can't discuss the timing because I think that would be inconsistent with my duty. But I just simply tell you that when people are interviewed, when things are done, depend on all the facts of the investigation. And I will remind you that approximately 25 people have been prosecuted, some 20 convicted, and many have cooperated.

Senator SPECTER. Well, Madam Attorney General, one concluding comment. I disagree with you decisively about these issues and this timing, and you may make whatever judgment you like as to your comments, but the Senate has very important congressional oversight responsibilities and we can comment, both officially and as citizens with our First Amendment rights. And we are dealing with matters, an election for the year 2000, which is a great deal more important for this country than any individual prosecution. Prosecutions pale even by congressional oversight on the enactment of legislation.

But I have expressed my views and you have expressed yours. Senator Torricelli.

Attorney General RENO. I would just simply say, Senator, you can tell me that I am wrong, but I will have greater confidence in your telling me I am wrong when you have all the facts.

Senator TORRICELLI. Mr. Chairman, I would like to actually ask several questions, but first I feel it necessary to return to my friend Senator Sessions' reading of the Vice President's email. The emails in question were written on March 15, 1996 from the scheduler to the Vice President. They refer to a scheduling matter on April 28th, some 6 weeks later.

Madam Attorney General, I would assume that the Vice President of the United States in the middle of a reelection campaign in a national campaign is far busier than I am. Would you concede his schedule is probably somewhat more full than your own at that period of the year?

The scheduler asks him a question by email about an event that he is invited to go to in New York at the same time as two fundraisers in California, one in San Jose, one in Los Angeles, 6 weeks later. There is no mention who is hosting it, no mention who is attending it, the word Buddhist, indeed, no nation in the world practicing the Buddhist faith is even mentioned. There are no details. There are two fundraisers in 6 weeks. The e-mail asks: Are you going to go to the fundraisers you have already accepted or the event in New York?

To suggest that this is some significant piece of evidence that the Vice President was aware he was going to a Buddhist fundraiser is somewhat taking liberty with the facts. This piece of paper would not establish that the Vice President indeed knew anything.

Second, the committee had the opportunity to hear from a Craig DeSantos. Are you familiar with Mr. Mansfield

Attorney General RENO. Yes.

Senator TORRICELLI. He seems to be a very fine man, and indeed he disagrees adamantly with your recommendation not to have an independent counsel. He disagreed with your judgment to bring the case to Washington, but said he had no reason to think it was anything but proper, and that it was a judgment call that was properly made.

In questioning Mr. Mansfield, the majority of the committee seemed to think it significant that Mr. Mansfield had begun a prosecution, an investigation of the Buddhist Temple case and the case was removed from Los Angeles to Washington. But, indeed, in the course of questioning Mr. Mansfield, the following became clear from memorandum written by Mr. DeSantos. Mr. DeSantos believed: A, Mr. Mansfield had too much of a workload to handle the case; B, he had not properly handled the Kim campaign finance case because he was focusing no—the was focusing on ancillary matters rather than the critical questions; third, there was a policy directive to be careful not to interfere with elections, and we were in the middle of a national campaign; fourth, Mr. Mansfield had alleged he had already prepared subpoenas and had begun the investigation. Actually, upon questioning and a review of memorandum, it is clear that, in fact, Mr. Mansfield had done nothing of the kind; he had issued no subpoenas, prepared no subpoenas, and done almost no investigations.

Therefore, the removal of the case from Los Angeles to Washington was with absolutely no practical impact on the case whatsoever, and significantly, as I suggested, Mr. Mansfield even testified that he did not take issue with the decision. I think that is significant since among all the people produced to testify before this committee, he was represented as the one who was going to disagree with your decisions the most. In fact, this disagreement did not exist.

Third, I would now like to read something into the record. Senator Specter and I have at great length read hundreds of memorandums, thousands of pages of testimony, and most of my colleagues have probably not had the opportunity. It might appear frightening to them, but I am going to read the entire text of Mr. La Bella's memorandum dealing with Vice President Gore.

Now, the light is on yellow, so this might seem impossible, and maybe I won't succeed. But I can accomplish this in 30 seconds, and not just because I am from New Jersey.

Here is the entire memorandum regarding the Vice President of the United States in this investigation: "During the investigation concerning Vice President Gore's fundraising calls from the White House, the Department concluded that he did not solicit hard money and, therefore, could be in no violation of 607. The fact is that Gore, using a credit card, placed several calls to the White House to pitch soft money contributions. The Vice President denied that he was aware that the soft money contributions were routinely being split between receipts by the DNC between soft and hard accounts. He stated in his interview that he did not recall the Ickes memo directed to him on the issues or the discussions at the regular Wednesday night meetings about this point. The Vice President's failure to recall reading the memo sent him is reminiscent of his claim not to have read the April 1996 memo advising him that he was to attend the Hacienda Heights, California, temple event. Quite apart from the 607 analysis, it is evident that to the extent that either the Common Cause allegations, conspiracy to defraud the United States, presents a viable potential violation of Federal law, the Vice President would certainly be among those whose conduct would be reviewed. Like President Clinton and Harold Ickes, he participated in the fundraising and strategic effort of the White House as they impacted the DNC and the Clinton-Gore 1996 campaign."

That, Madam Attorney General, as you are well aware, is the sum total of Mr. La Bella's recommendations, evidence, and allegations regarding the Vice President. This committee is led to believe that based on that analysis, your judgment not to appoint an independent counsel is somehow suspect, that this was not a judgment call upon which reasonable people could differ.

Mr. Radek, upon having read that memorandum, concluded the following: "The portion of the report devoted to Vice President Gore is only one-page long. It is so superficial that I am at a loss at to know how to proceed. Because we are offered no facts or analysis, I am unable to offer any views on this recommendation. With respect to the apparent criticism of the Attorney General's conclusion last year that the fundraising calls did not warrant appointment of independent counsel, the report makes no specific points. Thus, I am unable to even respond. Our conclusions that these were soft money solicitations and, thus, outside the scope of Section 607 was based on the results of hundreds of interviews with those who participated in the calls and the examination of scores of documents. In addition, as a wholly independent ground supporting our recommendation, we documented a well-established departmental policy of not prosecuting 607 violations absent aggravating circumstances not present here."

A great deal will be said in this committee; an enormous amount has been written. That is the conflict. Mr. Radek I think put it best: It was too simple, in my opinion too sophomoric, it presented no compelling evidence, nothing that should have denied you reaching the judgment you actually reached. Indeed, I believe Mr. Radek was kind.

That, Mr. Chairman, I am sure our colleagues are surprised to know, is what Mr. La Bella found after his investigation. That is the report. That is all that is before this committee.

Senator SPECTER. Well, I am going to take the liberty of the chairman for just less than minute to supplement what you read as to what Mr. La Bella wrote, because there is more. In addition, he wrote, "The type of analysis involved in determining whether the Vice President was part of the scheme to solicit soft money, knowing that it would be turned to hard money for the media campaign, is subjective and open to debate. By routinely embracing the most innocent inference at every turn, even if the inferences are factually indefensible, the memorandum creates an appearance that the Department is straining to avoid the appointment of an independent counsel and foreclose what many would characterize as an impartial review of the allegations. When you look at the facts, the memos, the messages, and the DNC practice, it is hard to say that there is only one conclusion to be reached, but there is a great deal more" than La Bella. There is Freeh, there is Parkinson, there is Litt, and now there is Senator Grassley.

Senator GRASSLEY. Well, first of all, Mr. Chairman, based on comments that the Attorney General made in response to my opening statement on the advice of counsel argument, I want to enter a document in the record as a counterresponse. I don't know if General Reno knows if you have had—if she has had a chance to review the FBI internal documents that they provided our subcommittee, but I think that these documents show that the FBI general counsel, as articulated by the Director, scoffed at the legitimacy of the advice of counsel argument. I believe that document is from Larry Parkinson. He is the FBI general counsel. And so I hope to pursue the issue of inserting that memo in the record to balance out the Attorney General's response. The document is located in S–407, and I have asked the staff to retrieve that, and I hope that we could put that in there to balance——

Senator SPECTER. Without objection, it will be made a part of the record.

[The letter follows:]

DECEMBER 4, 1998.

MEMORANDUM

To: Director Freeh.
From: Larry Parkinson.
Subject: Independent counsel matter: Potential election law violations involving President Clinton and Vice President Gore.

For purposes of your consultation with the Attorney General on the pending independent counsel matter, this memorandum is intended to summarize our discussions on the key issues. For the reasons stated below, it is appropriate to recommend that she seek the appointment of an independent counsel to investigate potential election law violations involving President Clinton and Vice President Gore. Because similar allegations have been made against the Dole presidential election campaign, the independent counsel should be authorized to investigate those allegations as well.

This memorandum is divided into two parts. The first section focuses primarily on the narrow question presented at the end of this 90-day preliminary inquiry: is the advice of counsel defense sufficient for the Attorney General to conclude by "clear and convincing evidence" that the President and Vice President lacked the requisite criminal intent? The second section discusses broader issues that justify the appointment of an independent counsel (regardless of the outcome on the narrow legal issue).

I. THE 90-DAY PRELIMINARY INQUIRY

A. *Threshold issues*

The Radek/Vicinanzo memorandum dated November 20, 1998 ("DOJ memo") streamlines the discussion by resolving correctly several important threshold issues. First, the memo defers appropriately to the FEC auditors' conclusion that the DNC-financed "issue ads" can be attributed to the Clinton/Gore campaign committee, thereby violating the spending limits. That conclusion obviously has been strengthened by this week's public release of the Audit Division's final report. The audit report, along with the very strong concurring opinion by the FEC Office of General Counsel, makes a compelling statement that the Clinton/Gore campaign illegally benefited from the media campaign.[1] Therefore, the basic facts that led to the initiation of the 90-day preliminary inquiry—the audit finding—have become stronger.[2]

The DOJ memo also resolves the issue of control, after setting forth a good factual summary of the genesis and development of the issue ad campaign. The memo correctly concludes that the ad campaign was controlled in all major respects by the White House:

> [T]here was little dispute that the DNC issue ad campaign was not only coordinated with the White House but controlled by it. Fowler described the White House control as "near absolute."

DOJ Memo at 29. Among many other things, the memo relies on the April 17, 1996 from memo from Ickes to Fowler establishing that all DCN expenditures were subject to prior White House approval.[3]

With respect to the purpose of the media campaign, the DOJ memo appears to give credence to the witness statements that the primary purpose of the issue ads was to aid the Democratic party and not to reelect the President. Such statements appear to be disingenuous at best; the documentary evidence clearly indicates that the primary purpose of the ads was the reelection of the President. In fact, the FED Audit Report takes the matter a step further: not only does it flatly reject the argument that the ads were not intended primarily to reelect the President, it essentially alleges an outright fraud:

> The Audit Division does not dispute that the advertisements in fact address pending political issues. However, the facts ascertained during the audit indicates that the primary purpose for addressing these issues was to assist President Clinton's reelection. It further appears that those facts which might otherwise demonstrate that the purpose and "targeting" of the advertisements were related to an overall party agenda (rather than the President's reelection) are true because of a *deliberate effort to conceal the actual purpose of the advertisements.*

FEC Audit Division Report on Clinton/Gore '96, at 42 (emphasis added).

Although its own analysis of "purpose" leaves something to be desired, the DOJ memo does reach a very significant conclusion: "it is clear that [President Clinton and Vice President Gore] both were sufficiently involved to be deemed coconspirators or aiders and abettors of any potential criminal violations of the FECA or PPMPAA." DOJ Memo at 31. This is an enormously significant conclusion in light of the FEC audit findings that there were violations of the relevant statutes. We are left, then, with the sole issue of whether the President and Vice President committed such violations "knowingly and willfully."

B. Advice of counsel defense

I view the advice of counsel defense as fairly strong in this case, but not strong enough to satisfy the "clear and convincing" standard under the Independent Counsel Act. I strongly disagree with the statement in the DOJ memo that "it is hard to imagine a more compelling set of facts establishing an advice-of-counsel defense." DOJ Memo at 40. While there appears to be no dispute that two of the lawyers representing the DNC and Clinton/Gore—Sandler and Utrecht—were involved significantly in the ad campaign process, the DOJ memo itself notes certain factors that cut against a viable advice of counsel defense.

1. No direct contact between lawyers and principals

The memo points out that where the attorneys never advise the principal clients directly, this undercuts to some degree the advise of counsel defense. It appears to be undisputed that the two experts, Sandler and Utrecht, never had direct contact

---

[1] As you know, the career FEC auditors and lawyers reached similar conclusions about the Dole campaign.

[2] The FEC Commissioners met in public session on December 3, 1998. Campcon had agents in attendance and has reported that several of the Commissioners appeared hostile to the Audit Report. As expected, the final resolution by the Commission is uncertain. One thing that does appear certain, however, is that there will be no resolution for at least several months. Thus, there appears to be little reason for the Attorney General to seek a 60-day extension of the preliminary investigation.

[3] This total White House control of DNC expenditures raises a significant legal issue. As you will recall, in our January 30, 1998 memorandum to DAG Holder, we argued strongly that this was a case about "control" and not mere "coordination." Based on their discussions with the FEC auditors and attorneys, our agents believe that the FEC has acquired only a fraction of the evidence that Campcon has obtained regarding "control." When asked how they would treat a situation in which there was total control of committee expenditures by a campaign, the FEC staff responded that it was an intriguing scenario with which they had never been faced.

with the President or Vice President. Instead, their advice filtered through intermediaries. The principal intermediary was Harold Ickes, who is, after all, the subject of a separate investigation for perjury. (While the perjury allegations are unrelated to media fund issue, does it make sense to shut down an investigation based on an advice of counsel defense where the person actually relaying the advice is about to have his own independent counsel?)

There appears to be relatively little evidence that actual legal advice was transmitted to the President or Vice President. Instead, this seems to be a situation in which the President and Vice President were told that "lawyers were involved" and that seemed to satisfy them. (See, e.g., DOJ memo at 40: "The Vice President felt confident that Quinn, who had some expertise in this area and was a good lawyer, had ensured that the ads were legal.") While certainly relevant to state of mind, this kind of evidence is not particularly persuasive in establishing a solid advice of counsel defense.

It also appears that the President and Vice President were relying primarily on Ickes and Quinn, even though they were not acting in a legal capacity. At the time, Ickes was Deputy Chief of Staff to the President and Quinn was Chief of Staff to the Vice President. The fact that they also happened to be lawyers does not necessarily mean they were dispensing "legal advice" for purposes of analyzing an advice of counsel defense.

Finally, there is one clear indication that the legal advice of Sandler and Utrecht may not have been getting through. As noted in footnote 11 of the DOJ memo (p. 22), "Sandler and Utrecht stated that they consistently applied the 'electioneering message' legal standard, not the express advocacy standard, when they reviewed the content of the DNC ads. Yet virtually every other witness recalls Sandler and Utrecht's advice in terms of express advocacy." While the memo concludes that this inconsistency is not significant, certainly it raises some question about whether the attorneys' advice was being heard and heeded.

2. The attorneys were not disinterested

The DOJ memo points out accurately that Sandler, as general counsel for the DNC, and Utrecht, as general counsel for the Clinton/Gore campaign committee, "worked for organizations with an unmistakable interest in ensuring the reelection of President Clinton," DOJ Memo at 38. The memo also states that "courts have declined to instruct juries on advice of counsel where the evidence indicated that the attorney was not disinterested in the outcome." Without impugning their integrity or professionalism,[4] Sandler and Utrecht certainly were not disinterested in the outcome.

3. No one sought advice from the FEC

If the DNC or Clinton/Gore truly wanted disinterested—and dispositive—advice on whether the spending for "issue ads" was properly allocated, they obviously could have gone to the FEC. They chose not to, presumably because they were afraid they might receive an answer they did not like. (When I met with the FEC's Chief Auditor in September 1998, he reacted viscerally when I asked him if the DNC or Clinton/Gore had ever sought advice on these matters.)

4. The Sandler memo

There is one clear indication that Sandler—one of the two lawyers critical to a viable advice of counsel defense—had doubts about whether the media campaign was violating the law. In a February 2, 1996 memo to Don Flowler, Sandler stated:

> Under (the FEC's legal) test, the DNC is bumping up right against *(and maybe a little bit over)* the line in running our media campaign about the federal budget debate, praising the President's plan and criticizing Dole by name.

(Emphasis added). When the same memo was sent to Ickes at the White House, it had been rewritten to state that the FEC's "electioneering message" test "is the standard we are applying (albeit aggressively) in the current DNC media campaign." When interviewed about these memos, Sandler gave a contorted explanation which led our agents to believe he was lying.

---

[4] Apparently both Utrecht and Sandler are recognized experts in the election law arena, which has very few practitioners. Utrecht in particular is a very impressive witness, according to the agents who interviewed her.

5. The investigation was by definition limited

As is true in any preliminary investigation conducted pursuant to the Independent Counsel Act, we conducted this 90-day inquiry[5] without the use of standard investigative tools. Therefore, we had to rely on voluntary production of documents, voluntary statements by witnesses, and agreed-upon attorney-client privilege waivers. While our agents felt that they received full document production from the DNC, they were not confident that all relevant White House documents had been produced. While I am unaware of any specific documents we believe to be missing, Campcon has had significant difficulties with White House document production since the Task Force began its work.

C. The "clear and convincing evidence" standard

Under all the circumstances, it is reasonable to conclude by "clear and convincing evidence" that the president and Vice President lacked the requisite state of mind? As we pointed out during deliberations on the recent Gore and Ickes matters, Congress clearly intended to set a very high threshold before an Attorney General could close a case, either before or after a preliminary investigation, on the ground that the subject lacked the state of mind necessary to commit the alleged crime. In 1987, Congress amended the Independent Counsel Act in an effort to curb what it viewed as a "disturbing" practice by the Department:

> A third problem with the Department of Justice's implementation of the statute is its practice in several cases to decline further proceedings, despite specific information from a credible source of possible wrongdoing, due to a lack of evidence of the subject's criminal intent. The decision not to proceed has sometimes been made even in the face of conflicting or inconclusive evidence on the subject's state of mind.

> *　　*　　*　　*　　*　　*　　*

> The Justice Department's demand for proof of criminal intent to justify continuing independent counsel cases is disturbing, because criminal intent is extremely difficult to assess, especially in the early stages of an investigation. Further, it often requires subjective judgments, which should ideally be left to an independent decisionmaker. It is not the type of factual question that the Attorney General's limited role in the independent counsel process and lack of access to important investigative tools such as grand juries and subpoenas.

1987 U.S.C.C.A.N. at 2159–60.

The 1987 conference agreement emphasized, "The conferees believe it will be a *rare case* In which the Attorney General will be able to meet the clear and convincing standard and in which such evidence would be clear on its face. It would be unusual for the Attorney General to compile sufficient evidence at that point in the process." *Id.* At 2190 (emphasis added).

The question is whether this is one of those "rare cases." We should bear in mind the accurate conclusion that the President and Vice President "both were sufficiently involved to be deemed coconspirators or aiders and abettors of any potential criminal violations of the FEC or PPMPAA," DOJ memo at 31. There was a conscious, well-orchestrated effort by the White House to evade the spending limits through the media campaign. Moreover, this kind of campaign was unprecedented, as the President readily acknowledged when he bragged to his supporters about how he had found a new way to spend enormous amounts of money for the campaign. Under all the circumstances, notwithstanding the potentially viable advice of counsel defense, this matter should not be closed on a "clear and convincing" finding.

II. BROADER ISSUES: CONFLICT OF INTEREST

Even if the Attorney General determines that there is "clear and convincing" evidence of a lack of intent in this 90-day matter, she should step back and consider the impact of closing this investigation. It would be fair to summarize the decision in the following way:

—For two years, the investigators advocated a need to conduct a broad investigation of the entire campaign financing scheme conducted by the White House and the DNC, including both the raising of campaign money and the spending of that money. The media campaign was critical to the reelection and many of the apparent

---

[5] In fact, because of the deadlines required for preparation and review of the DOJ memo and subsequent deliberations, the actual investigation was approximately 60 days.

criminal abuses resulted from the need to keep the money flowing into the media fund.

—For nearly two years, investigation of the media fund was largely off-limits while the Department debated internally about the scope of the campaign finance laws and whether we should defer to the FEC. In the meantime, the Task Force pursued a variety of individual cases largely independent of one another.

—While we were debating internally on the broader issues, the FEC was actually working on a comprehensive audit of the two presidential campaigns (much to our surprise). Contrary to the prevailing view within DOJ, the FEC auditors found massive violations of the law by both presidential campaigns.

—Faced with evidence of legal violations, the Department was forced to initiate a preliminary investigation under the Independent Counsel Act.

—The preliminary investigation consisted primarily (but not exclusively) of an examination of an advice of counsel defense. We went to the subjects and their lawyers and asked them what happened. They informed us that the subjects had no criminal intent, notwithstanding the apparent violations. After investigating that issue, we agreed with the subjects and closed the entire matter, with one exception:

—The exception is the related investigation of the Dole campaign. Since we have no evidence relating to an advice of counsel defense for that campaign, we will keep that investigation alive, particularly in light of the FEC's recent Audit Report.

The media fund/Common Cause allegations have always been the biggest piece of the campaign finance scandal. In large part, those allegations led to the creation of the Campcon Task Force in the first instance. Nevertheless, those allegations have never been investigated in any comprehensive or organized way. Nearly a year ago (January 1998), we sent a detailed memorandum to the Department seeking a comprehensive investigation of the Common Cause allegations. In that memo, we stated:

> "[T]he Common Cause allegations are the most serious of those issues raised in connection with the investigation of campaign finance." In a series of well-researched submissions, Common Cause has described a scheme to circumvent the FECA and presidential funding laws on a breathtaking scale. For knowing and willful violations of these laws, Congress provided for criminal penalties.
>
> It has been nearly 16 months since Common Cause first brought these allegations to the attention of DOJ. The Department has on more than one occasion written to Common Cause stating that the Task Force is "reviewing a variety of campaign financing issues arising out the last national election" and is "examining" the soft money issues raised by Common Cause. In fact, the Task Force has undertaken no actual investigation of these allegations. Consequently, some of the most fundamental questions relating to the 1995–96 presidential campaign remain outstanding:
> —How were the campaign funds raised?
> —How were they spent?
> —How were they allocated and reported for FECA purposes?
> —Who made the fundraising and spending decisions?
> While the Task Force has uncovered partial answers to these questions, in particular the last one, it is not because we have addressed them in any systematic investigative fashion. Instead, our information has come primarily from Common Cause, the newspapers, and tangentially from our investigation of other matters.

Very little has changed in the last year. After several months of memos and discussions last winter, in February the Attorney General took under advisement the matter of whether the Common Cause allegations could be investigated. We never received a response until July of 1998, when we read (with great surprise) the Attorney General's congressional testimony in which she stated that the Department was deferring to the FEC.[6]

Our January 1998 memorandum also recommended the immediate appointment of an independent counsel:

---

[6] In April 1998, the Task Force investigators developed a investigative plan and dubbed it the "Media Fund" plan. Because it was never clear how the Task Force could investigative the "media fund" while steering clear of the Common Cause allegations, the investigative plan was necessarily truncated. In any event, beginning in May, the investigators began to conduct the "media fund" investigation and obtained a significant amount of information that became very useful during the current 90-day preliminary investigation. That investigation consisted primarily of interviews of state party officials in a dozen key battleground states (focusing on the use of the state parties as conduits for the DNC), document production by the media consultants, and interviews of three DNC employees (Brad Marshall and two lower-level employees).

Because the Common Cause allegations clearly involve the President, they must be investigated by an Independent Counsel. Moreover, the Attorney General should seek the appointment of an Independent Counsel immediately. Since the Department has had the allegations for nearly 16 months, a preliminary inquiry does not appear to be an option. Finally, we once again would incorporate by reference the FBI's prior written submissions recommending that, independent of the mandatory provision of the Independent Counsel statute, the Attorney General should exercise her discretionary authority pursuant to the political conflict of interest provision.

Notwithstanding the passage of time, our arguments remain the same. If anything, the need for investigation has increased. Intentionally or not, the Department has deferred to the FEC, which has spoken publicly in a resounding way.

For nearly two years, the Department has been investigating the potential criminal conduct of the President and Vice President. That is an inherent conflict of interest that the Independent Counsel Act was designed to address. Even if the Attorney General concludes by "clear and convincing evidence" discretionary authority and seek the appointment of an independent counsel.

Attorney General RENO. Do you have that, sir?

Senator GRASSLEY. Yes, I think we do have it.

Attorney General RENO. May I see it, please?

Senator GRASSLEY. Oh, we have it in 407.

Senator SPECTER. I think we can provide a copy momentarily. That is a subject that I intend to ask the Attorney General about.

Senator GRASSLEY. Well, since I have asked the staff to get that—we do not have it, so we would request then that that be given to us so we can include it in the record.

Senator SPECTER. Well, I am sure we can obtain it. All of those documents have been released into the public domain.

Attorney General RENO. I would refer you to page 3 of a memorandum from Larry Parkinson to Director Freeh. "I view the advice of counsel defense as fairly strong in this case, but not strong enough to satisfy the 'clear and convincing' standard under the Independent Counsel Act."

Senator GRASSLEY. OK.

Attorney General RENO. That is somewhat at odds with whatever document you have, sir, and I would like to see it, please.

Senator GRASSLEY. Okay. Well——

Senator SPECTER. Well, we will get to that. Mr. Parkinson in that memorandum——

Attorney General RENO. I am just—let me deal with Senator Grassley. All I am trying to say is he read something to me. I have a Parkinson memo on this issue. I would like to be able to see what you are reading from so that I might appropriately respond, since it does not seem to be what I have.

Senator SPECTER. Well, we will be glad to make that document available to you. But——

Attorney General RENO. May I make—because you I know you have this, and I do trust that you will look at it and note that he viewed the advice of counsel defense as strong.

Senator SPECTER. Well, the memorandum by Mr. Parkinson goes into some detail in dismissing the advice of counsel argument on a number of grounds: first, that the two lawyers, Joseph Sandler and Lynn Utrecht were not disinterested parties. Mr. Sandler was general counsel for the DNC, and Mr. Utrecht or Lynn Utrecht was general counsel for the Clinton-Gore campaign.

He further dismisses the advice of counsel argument on the ground that those lawyers did not give their advice directly to the

President and Vice President, but to intervening individuals, Mr. Ickes and Mr. Quinn, who were not disinterested parties.

And, finally, he dismisses the advice of counsel argument on the ground that there was a reservation by Mr. Sandler who said, "Under the test, the DNC is bumping up right against and maybe a little bit over the line." So that as you accurately quote, Attorney General Reno, he does say that it doesn't satisfy the clear and convincing evidence test, but Mr. Parkinson thoroughly debunks the advice of counsel defense in his written memorandum.

Attorney General RENO. No, Senator, I would take issue with you. He does not debunk it. He calls it fairly strong. What he says is: I can't meet the clear and convincing evidence test that the statute requires for showing intent. But he does not address the points made in 6 through the end of the notification to the court, and I would ask that Senator Grassley be given a copy of it so that he can understand the lengths that we went to, the law that we considered, and I will be happy to make this available to him if it is not with the committee.

Senator SPECTER. Well, we are going to get into the point a little later in detail. Whether you agree with the conclusion that he debunks it or not, he conclusively comes to the judgment that it was not sufficient to reject the appointment of independent counsel. Wouldn't you agree with that, Attorney General Reno?

Attorney General RENO. Let me get it for you again and just go over the points so that you can understand.

Senator SPECTER. Well, I do understand, and Mr. Parkinson comes to the conclusion——

Attorney General RENO. Well, he certainly didn't debunk it——

Senator SPECTER. Excuse me. I want to finish my sentence. That the defense of advice of counsel does not constitute clear and convincing evidence to negate the requisite intent. Isn't that correct?

Attorney General RENO. He says, "I view the advice of counsel defense as fairly strong in this case, but not strong enough to satisfy the 'clear and convincing' standard under the Independent Counsel Act."

Senator SPECTER. That is what I said.

Attorney General RENO. He and I disagree on that, and we have set forth our position and I think made it very clear.

Senator SPECTER. Well, I understand you disagree. The point was whether Mr. Parkinson found the clear and—found the advice of counsel argument sufficient to reject——

Attorney General RENO. He did not find it sufficient, as I pointed out, but neither did he debunk it.

Senator SPECTER. Well, I think the point has been made. He said that the argument did not support your conclusion that independent counsel should not be appointed.

Attorney General RENO. I was responding to Senator Grassley's comment that indicated that he did not think the advice of counsel defense was very strong.

Senator SPECTER. Senator Grassley and I have passed the 20-year test. We help each other out occasionally.

Senator Grassley.

Attorney General RENO. I don't think Senator Grassley needs anybody to help him. I have found him very constructive and very thoughtful and an excellent advocate.

Senator GRASSLEY. Now, we will have to end this right here by my saying to you that we are going to pursue that document from S–407, get that to you, and if we—we may have to do it by our response in writing, but we will give you a chance to respond to that.

Attorney General RENO. Thank you, sir.

Senator GRASSLEY. I think I might have time for a couple of questions, and I am well aware of your admonition that I should be appreciative of Mr. Radek's work, as you are.

Attorney General RENO. Could I just say something? Everybody has been calling him Mr. "Ra-dek." It is Mr. "Ray-dek."

Senator GRASSLEY. Well, Mr. Radek. Now, going on from that point, we are talking about the same person.

I want to ask you a question, and that is in reference to the fact that I had made reference to an inspectors general meeting and how a U.S. attorney had offered their services as an alternative to career investigators trying to present evidence of misconduct against high-ranking officials. I was wondering if you were aware of the feeling among at least some U.S. Attorneys—and there was only one U.S. Attorney at this meeting that spoke about this—of the frustration with the Public Integrity Section. And were you aware of that Public Integrity Section's reputation?

Attorney General RENO. I am aware of their reputation of calling it like they see it, of looking at all the evidence, of not jumping to conclusions, of making the best judgment they can. I am also away, after 22 years as a prosecutor, that nothing can get an investigator more upset than somebody that tells them you need to get more evidence, and that there is an inevitable tension and conflict. And I think it is important that we look at each case.

I have met with the inspectors general, talking about how we can build better lines of communication. I have worked with the U.S. Attorneys in the Criminal Division to make sure that there is coordination between them and that some of the tension that exists be resolved by establishing direct lines of communication and understanding what is necessary.

Senator GRASSLEY. On another point, but still in regard to Mr. Radek, at a previous hearing he had expressed his displeasure with the independent counsel. So my question to you is: Did he ever express his displeasure with the independent counsel statute to you?

Attorney General RENO. Yes.

Senator GRASSLEY. Then my question to you is: How did you weigh that in your decision?

Attorney General RENO. Well—do we have that?

Apparently, when the Independent Counsel Act was being considered, for example, in 1981, the then Associate Attorney General Rudolph Giuliani testified before the Senate Committee on Governmental Affairs urging that the action be repealed. He said, "The system depends quite properly on the integrity of the Department of Justice personnel. The assumption upon which the special prosecutor law is premised, that the Department of Justice should not be trusted to investigate or prosecute certain Federal offenses, is simply unfounded."

I think I relied on Lee Radek like the administration at the time relied on Rudy Giuliani as a vigorous prosecutor.

Senator GRASSLEY. And so then the bottom line of that is that Mr. Radek's view of the independent counsel law and the fact that he didn't like that was in no way—or you saw that in no way of lessening his opinion about whether or not there ought to be an investigation or counsel——

Attorney General RENO. There are so many things that come up where people disagree and still carry out the law and do it the right way.

Senator SPECTER. Thank you very much, Senator Grassley.

Senator KYL.

Senator TORRICELLI. Mr. Chairman, if I could ask how we are going to proceed here, the Democratic Party obviously would like to continue to be heard in this rotation.

Senator SPECTER. All they have to do is appear and they will be heard, as the court crier says all the time.

Senator TORRICELLI. Previously we have been alternating a balance, regardless of the number of people who were here on each side. Is it your intention now to proceed entirely with the Republican side before returning——

Attorney General RENO. While you are deciding that, may I take a break?

Senator SPECTER. Yes, of course. We will take a 10-minute break.

[Recess 4:38 to 4:47 p.m.]

Senator SPECTER. We will turn to Senator Sessions.

Senator SESSIONS. Senator Torricelli and I have talked about this email matter, and he raised a point of interest, skillfully, as he always does. I would note that the e-mail I had reference to was dated March 15 from his assistant to Vice President Gore saying that Rabbi Grossman has invited you to appear to give the keynote address at the rabbinical counsel in New York. Then she went on to say, "This is the same evening you wanted to fly out to California and do the two fundraisers in San Jose and L.A."—Los Angeles—"while Sarah and Mrs. Gore visit colleges."

So I would just say that responds directly to his inquiry and direction about the fundraisers, and she said further, "We have confirmed those two fundraisers for Monday, April 29."

Then the Vice President the next day, March 16, responds, "If we have already booked the fundraisers, then we have to decline." And there were two that day, the San Jose and the temple fundraiser. And I must note that that appears to be the 16th, the day after the Vice President, as I recall the facts, met with John Huang, Maria Hsia, and the temple master in the White House. And I would suggest it would be quite likely that they would have discussed on that day that a fundraiser was to occur in the Buddhist temple fundraiser, at least in Los Angeles. It is a matter that does not prove a criminal case. It is a matter that I would suggest that provides some credence to the fact that the Vice President would have known this was a fundraiser; would you not agree, Attorney General Reno?

Attorney General RENO. I will not comment, sir. I do not think it is right to comment on a pending investigation before all of the facts are in, and I shall not.

Senator SESSIONS. I appreciate that and respect that. Our problem here is that the Executive Branch has exclusive prosecutorial responsibility and since we have given up the independent counsel procedure, there is no other procedure for that. So I think it is particularly legitimate, under this new time, that the Congress watch closely when the Executive Branch is called upon to investigate itself. And that is why I justify Senator Specter's concern about this and desire to have a hearing. And I am not asking you to say what you cannot say, but I do believe that it is a matter of utmost importance and that the American people need to have complete confidence in this procedure.

Attorney General RENO. And I do urge you to watch carefully.

Senator SESSIONS. The matter that really has caused me distress and to lose some confidence in what has taken place so far with regard to this investigation and its late ripening was what occurred in 1996, Attorney General Reno. That is when Assistant U.S. Attorney Mansfield prepared, at least initially, some papers toward commencing an investigation of the temple fundraiser after he read about it in the newspaper. Of course, he had successfully convicted Republican Congressman Kim on campaign finance matters, and he saw this arise in the newspaper and begin to take some steps toward proceeding with it. Perhaps there was a misunderstanding about whether he actually issued subpoenas, but we saw the paperwork where he had commenced the paperwork toward issuing subpoenas.

And I guess my question to you is, well, before he got very far toward that end, he received a directive, verbal and written, from Mr. Radek to stop the investigation, that Mr. Radek and Public Integrity was taking it over. Were you aware that that directive had gone out to stop that investigation?

Attorney General RENO. I was aware that they were trying to do everything they could to make sure that any case that might be subject to the Independence Counsel Act be appropriately considered.

Senator SESSIONS. So you basically understood that Los Angeles would be stopped from what they were doing and that Public Integrity would take it over.

Attorney General RENO. That is correct.

Senator SESSIONS. Were you aware that from the date that Public Integrity took that over—well, let me back up. One of the things that triggered that, if you will recall, was a letter from Senator McCain and five Congressmen requesting an independent prosecutor, listing some concerns. Part of that was the Buddhist Temple fundraiser that they listed. Do you recall that?

Attorney General RENO. I recall the 5-star letter, sir.

Senator SESSIONS. Yes. And that is what triggered, as I understand it, Mr. Radek's and your decision to intervene and take it over. Were you aware that after it was taken over that no subpoenas were issued, no witnesses were interviewed, no records were obtained from the Buddhist Temple fundraiser, and that the recommendation Mr. Radek made to you to decline an independent counsel at that time was based solely on newspaper articles and maybe the letter from the Senators and Congressmen?

Attorney General RENO. I do not know to what you are referring, sir.

Senator SESSIONS. Well, in our hearings, Mr. Radek testified that he did not conduct any investigation, did not interview any witnesses, and did not obtain any records, as the assistant U.S. attorney in California had planned to do, but yet he still made a recommendation that there was no basis for an independent counsel. And my question is did you know he had conducted no investigation to obtain any information?

Attorney General RENO. I do not think so, sir. If you have the language from—if you have the transcript, I will take a look at it and try to understand it better.

Senator SESSIONS. I hope you would because, to me, Mr. Mansfield, the experienced prosecutor in California, testified that he was very concerned and actually had a contentious telephone call or two with the Public Integrity Section, in which he expressed concern that witnesses would disappear, that records could be destroyed. And we know, since that time, that a number of the witnesses have left the country, that Ted Sioeng has left the country, a man whom the Vice President was sitting next to at this fundraiser, that one of the nuns admitted destroying evidence "because we did not want to embarrass the Vice President," and that the video of the event was never obtained.

Are you familiar with those circumstances?

Attorney General RENO. No, sir. What I am familiar with is a letter to Congressman Gilman, dated November 29, 1996, in which he said, "Mark Richard wrote saying the issues raised in your letter, taken as a whole, are extraordinarily complex, both factually and legally, and warrant careful consideration. Indeed, public interest organizations, the press, members of Congress and the public have recently expressed concerns about campaign financing practices by both parties in the recent national election. As a result of these serious and legitimate concerns, a task force has been created within the Public Integrity Section of the Criminal Division, composed of career Federal prosecutors, to explore fully the range of allegations and issues that have been raised. The task force will determine which, if any, warrant criminal investigation or any other action by either the Department or an independent counsel and will conduct, with the assistance of the appropriate investigative agencies, any criminal investigations that are warranted."

My understanding is that the Temple matter was thoroughly investigated by the task force, and if we, at that time, had uncovered any information that showed that there was specific and credible information that a covered person may have committed a crime, we would have triggered the Independent Counsel Act.

Senator SESSIONS. But what happened was, just to be clear, in Mark Richards' letter that you just referred to, on Page 1, the last paragraph, says, "We reviewed your letter * * *" that is to the Congressman "* * * as well as press reports and correspondence we have received."

But it indicates pretty plainly that they did nothing else, and this was the 30-day preliminary inquiry period that, it seems to me, quite important that that investigation should have initiated, key witnesses should have been interviewed, documents should have been obtained, if possible, and then we would have been in a lot better position to make a decision than based on press reports; would you not agree?

Attorney General RENO. I think that there are certain thresholds for investigation. And I think before we trigger the preliminary investigation, that we have got to have specific and credible evidence.

Senator SESSIONS. Well, what we do know is that, later on, the Vice President was interviewed a little over a year later and a decision was made, apparently at the highest levels, not to ask about the Buddhist Temple matter. And it was only 4 years later, after this assistant United States attorney had been prepared to investigate, that the Vice President was even asked about it, and that was just a few months ago. And it was after that that Mr. Conrad has now concluded a person outside the Department should be called upon to conduct this investigation, pursuant to your procedures for a special counsel.

I guess my time has expired, but if you would like to comment on that——

Attorney General RENO. Yes, I would. Mr. Conrad, and Mr. La Bella before him, and Mr. Vicinanzo have conducted the investigation in the manner that they thought was best. And I am not talking about the Independent Counsel Act. I cannot talk about the course of a pending investigation. I do not think that is right or proper to try something in a committee hearing, as opposed to a court. But I feel very strongly that all three men are very able prosecutors and made their best judgment. I cannot control the timing of an investigation because I cannot control the course of trial dates, appeals and the like. But I am committed to making sure that justice is done promptly and swiftly, no matter what the ultimate result is.

Senator SESSIONS. Well, you have a lot of responsibilities, but I believe your staff, and we have had indepth hearings about it, failed you. And in a sense, you failed to supervise, in making that declination of independent counsel at that early date without even commencing any investigation. I think that was an error, and that has caused us to be at this late stage, and also has caused me to believe that the American public have a greater interest in having a special outside counsel conducting this than an inhouse counsel.

Attorney General RENO. I know you feel that way, sir. If circumstances justify the appointment of a special counsel, I will be the first person to do it.

Senator SESSIONS. Thank you very much.

Senator SPECTER. Attorney General Reno, we have brought down the memo, and I will be glad to make a copy of it available to you, on Parkinson. Let me know preliminarily that.

It starts off under the "Advice of Counsel Section" as follows: "I view the advice of counsel defense as fairly strong in this case, but not strong enough to satisfy the 'clear and convincing' standard under the Independent Counsel Act."

You read the part about it viewing it as strong. But then he goes on to say, "I strongly disagree with the statement in the DOJ memo * * *" that is your memo "* * * that it 'is hard to imagine a more compelling set of facts establishing an advice of counsel defense.'"

The "clear and convincing" test was put into effect in the Independent Counsel statute with the Congress in 1987 because thenAttorney General Meese was declining independent counsel on the ground of state of mind. So the Congress took a look at it, and the legislative history is clear, but even beyond the legislative history, the statute says that there have to be clear and convincing evidence of no criminal intent in order to rule out appointment of independent counsel.

We are going to take a break in just a few minutes. A vote has been called at 5 o'clock. We will give you a chance to read this.

Attorney General RENO. That is what I have been reading from, sir, and that is what I would like to respond to.

Senator SPECTER. Go ahead.

Attorney General RENO. Okay. It is going to take some time. So if you want to wait until you come back, I——

Senator SPECTER. Well——

Attorney General RENO. I want to go through the entire defense.

Senator SPECTER. All right. I would prefer, in the 4 minutes or so that I have left, to come back to a couple of questions which were pending on how many witnesses there were who provided evidence on hard money. In your statement, you say "only two——"

Attorney General RENO. Which case are you talking about, sir?

Senator SPECTER. Hard money, the question about whether the Vice President knew that——

Attorney General RENO. Are you talking about the second notification with respect to the preliminary investigation?

Senator SPECTER. I am referring to the notification, which you signed on August 26, 1998.

Attorney General RENO. OK, sir.

Senator SPECTER. It is a closed matter. And at Page 9, and you have referred to this, "Only two of the fifteen attendees at the meeting even recall the topic of a hardmoney component to the media fund being raised during the meeting."

Now, the evidence showed that there were four witnesses who made statements to the FBI regarding the hard money. Leon Panetta, White House chief of staff, said there was, among other things, "There was always a discussion and examination of the overall DNC budget and, at a minimum, a reference to the hard/soft breakdown in the media fund." Recalls the Vice President being there for all of these discussions as part of gearing up the reelection campaign. Meetings were structured around presentation to the President and to the Vice President.

And on your point that there was lack of focus, and I commented on this before, Mr. Panetta was quoted as saying, "Make sure they knew what the hell was going on."

Now, David Marshall, "recalled general discussion regarding the media campaign, including how much the DNC had spent to date and how much hard money was needed and how much soft money was needed to fund the media campaign."

Brian Bailey, specifically, "he recalls individuals discussing hard/soft money at the November 21, 1995, meeting," and that is the one that the President attended.

Now, when you disagree with what David Strauss provided because he had made contemporaneous notes of the November 21st meeting, 65-percent soft and 35-percent hard, it may be true that he has no independent recollection, did not testify, but his recollection was recorded, I do not think there is any doubt that that is evidence. Whether he remembers it or not, if he has prior recollection recorded, that is admissible evidence.

So my question to you: Is it not a fact that there were not two of the fifteen attendees, but there were three who recalled, and a fourth provided evidence in the form of prior recollection recorded?

Attorney General RENO. My understanding is that there were two who recalled the discussion, that a Mr. Bailey did not say he remembered the statements; rather, when shown Strauss's notes, he said they might be referring to hard/soft split of funding for the media fund, but had no memory of the statement.

Senator SPECTER. Can you speak into the microphone, please.

Attorney General RENO. The other person cited by Mr. Parkinson, Strauss, also had no memory of the discussion of the issues.

Senator SPECTER. But is it not true that Strauss had recorded his prior recollection?

Attorney General RENO. That is correct. But the issue is what was remembered, what was heard, what was understood, what was remembered.

Senator SPECTER. Is not the issue what evidence there was, not what was remembered?

Attorney General RENO. I am looking——

Senator SPECTER. If there is prior recollection recorded, is that not evidence?

Attorney General RENO. I am looking for evidence of what the Vice President heard, understood and remembered.

Senator SPECTER. Well, let us focus on——

Attorney General RENO. Because I cannot prosecute when I cannot prove a willful and——

Senator SPECTER. Well, let us focus on this for just a minute, and I am going to come to the point as to whether the standard was what you could prosecute on because I do not think that is the standard under the——

Attorney General RENO. That is not the standard, sir. The standard, what I concluded in this instance was, "Thus, I do not believe—the evidence I do not believe provides reasonable grounds to believe that further investigation of this matter is warranted. Notably, others attending the meeting also left it with an inaccurate understanding of the funding of the media campaign. The range of impressions and vagueness of understandings among all of the meeting attendees is striking and undercuts any reasonable inference that mere attendance at the meeting should have served to communicate to the Vice President an accurate understanding of the facts."

Senator SPECTER. I am going to come back to that, as I say, as to what the prosecution standard was.

But for just a moment, I want to focus on what is evidence. You proceed on evidence. Now, it may be a recollection, where a witness would testify as to what the witness recollected. But when David Strauss had a contemporaneous memorandum which says, "65-percent soft/35-percent hard," that is prior recollection recorded. And that is admissible evidence, is it not?

Attorney General RENO. I need to prove—I need evidence that shows what the Vice President heard, what he understood and what he recollected. Just because David Strauss heard something, does not mean the Vice President heard it.

Senator SPECTER. Well, of course it does not. But it raises an inference that if David Strauss is in a meeting with the Vice President and heard something, that the Vice President heard it. It does not prove it, but a jury could find it.

Attorney General RENO. And if David Strauss does not remember——

Senator SPECTER. Well, that is what I am focusing on. He does not have to remember, Attorney General Reno, if he has prior recollection recorded. Evidence in a court of law is satisfied by prior recollection recorded, as well as by current recollection as to what he heard. Are you denying that as a basic evidentiary rule?

Attorney General RENO. I am talking about if you want evidence in as to David Strauss's memory, that is one thing. I am trying to prove what the Vice President remembered.

Senator SPECTER. OK.

Senator TORRICELLI. Mr. Chairman, may I make an inquiry here? We are in the middle now of a vote in the Senate. There are going to be three successive votes on the Senate floor. The Attorney General has been here now for 3 hours and 8 minutes. I would appreciate a moment to say before I leave, I hope it would not be the committee's intention to keep her here by herself for an hour while we go with these votes, since she has been through several rounds of questioning. But in any case, Mr. Chairman, now in this round, you have addressed her for 10 minutes. I would like a moment, before we break to go to the vote, and it would be my hope then that the Attorney General would have the option of leaving at this point, in fairness to her, after so many hours of cooperative testimony.

How would you like to proceed?

Senator SPECTER. Well, if you wish to question now, I would be glad to defer to you. And what I would suggest—well, I would ask the Attorney General are you willing to stay longer?

Attorney General RENO. Are you going to keep me waiting for an hour?

Senator SPECTER. No. What I would plan to do is to leave here at about 5:18, go and vote and come back

Attorney General RENO. How long?

Senator SPECTER. About 10 minutes.

Attorney General RENO. How long after that? Because I have a——

Senator SPECTER. About 15 minutes.

Attorney General RENO. When do you think you will conclude?

Senator SPECTER. Before 6 o'clock.

Attorney General RENO. OK.

Senator SPECTER. Senator Torricelli.

Senator TORRICELLI. Thank you.

Madam Attorney General, thank you very much for your——

Attorney General RENO. I will have to leave at 6:00, Senator, because I do have a meeting.

Senator SPECTER. I am going to leave now and come back, and it will abbreviate the time.

Attorney General RENO. OK.

Senator TORRICELLI. Which makes me the only Democratic chairman of a committee in the entire Congress of the United States, Madam Attorney General. This is an enormously powerful situation. [Laughter.]

I, actually, for the record, first, wanted to clear up several things. Indeed, from the testimony the committee has heard in recent weeks, your recollection, Madam Attorney General, is correct. Indeed, Mr. Strauss only recalled the hard-money discussion on his third interview. There are only two people who remembered it initially, leaving thirteen who did not. And it is important that the record reflect that.

Second, it is important Senator Sessions should know that on the schedule for that day, it may well be that the e-mails indicated the Vice President was going to a fundraiser on the 29th. They do not indicate whose it was or anything about a Buddhist Temple. But more significantly, the Buddhist Temple event was at 1:30 p.m. Indeed, at 6:30 p.m. that night, he did have a meeting with the Finance Committee Steering Committee at the DNC. That is not in dispute. So, if the e-mails suggested a fundraiser on the 29th, it was correct, but it was not necessarily the Buddhist Temple event.

Third, Senator Specter, I am sure did not, in any way, intend to mislead the committee. But I read earlier from the La Bella memorandum of July 16, 1998, an excerpt, a single page dealing with Vice President Gore. I read that into the record to give credence to Mr. Radek's conclusion that the memorandum was I think his term was simplistic; in any case, that it consisted of a single page and was not enough of a foundation for the naming of an independent counsel.

Senator Specter read an additional excerpt. It is important for the record to note that is not from the La Bella memorandum of July 16. It does not have anything to do with the July 16th memorandum of Mr. La Bella. It was written at a later time in response to the Justice Department's decision, and there is no evidence that that was part of your deliberations or your decision-making process. I know he did not want to mislead the committee, but I do think it is important the record make clear my point stands. There was one page of analysis with regard to the Vice President. And as Mr. Radek suggested, it was very simple in its analysis.

Third, I would like to conclude by returning to Senator Feingold's point. Madam Attorney General, it is too late for the 1996 elections. And people in both parties have regrets how they were conducted, and there were mistakes made, not simply by the President, and the Vice President or Senator Dole, but indeed in many congressional elections. The laws are not being respected. There are problems. People in our country are not regarding them properly.

It is too late for 1996. It is not too late for 2000. The burden is primarily on this Congress, which has failed to meet its responsibility with comprehensive campaign finance reform. That is our problem, and we should be answerable to the American people for it. It is a breakdown of congressional responsibility.

But there is something additional in the Justice Department. While the Congress should be making clear that 527 organizations, as identified in the tax code, should not be used for blatant political purposes, coordinated with campaigns, misused by organizations, they are not only a policy problem—in my judgment, they are a legal problem.

And I would hope that at this point if the Campaign Finance Task Force and the Justice Department can make a great contribution, it is not correcting the past in 1996, it is also helping to deal with the 2000 elections. These organizations are illegal. They are improper deductions from people's taxes, conduits for private, corporate and even foreign money in the electoral process. They are being coordinated with campaigns. And after the 2000 elections, Madam Attorney General, it is going to be too late. People are going to win or lose elections based on the misuse of the tax code for these purposes. And just because the Congress has failed, does not mean the Justice Department has to fail. I hope you will take that under consideration.

Now, as a closing point, I only want to leave you then with this: I actually, unlike my colleagues, do not fault Senator Specter for revealing what was told to him about the interview of the Vice President. That was his judgment. But there is another matter. The choice between George W. Bush and Al Gore should be made in a debate between the candidates, not a debate between leaks from the Justice Department and statements by the Vice President. This cannot happen again, and it is wrong.

You will make your judgments, the Department will make its own judgments. They should be done privately, and they should be done so on the merits. This situation should not repeat itself. And I do not believe this is a failure of policy. It is a violation of the law. FBI agents were present at the Vice President's interview. The Vice President was placed under oath. Both of those must have been in contemplation if there was a future grand jury or a legal proceeding.

As you know from the case of the Office of Independent Counsel in the Lewinsky matter, in the rulings of the United States Court of Appeals, a matter likely to be presented, in the words of the Court, to a grand jury is a Rule 6(e) violation. It is a felony.

I do not know how it is done. I do not pretend to be giving advice on how you administer the Justice Department. But, Madam Attorney General, someone has let the Department down. Someone has violated the laws of the United States in revealing information that should have belonged to you and your associates alone—not the media, not me, not this committee, not any partisan political activity. Someone let you down. I hope that you are vigorous in finding out how that happened, whether it is polygraphing people who had access to the information, whether it is taking their statements. I do not know who it is.

And indeed, unlike some of the committee, I have a great regard for Mr. Conrad. He seems to be a man of integrity. I believe he is a serious man. He is entitled to have views that differ from me and differ from you. I think he is a good man. But someone who had access to his thinking and the things that he was writing, did not do right by the Department of Justice.

Madam Attorney General, thank you very much for your testimony today. No one, under the cruel and—unusual cruel and punishment provisions of the Constitution should be held before this committee for 3 hours and 15 minutes. You were great to do so.

Attorney General RENO. Thank you, sir.

Senator TORRICELLI. And now for the first time in this Congress, as a Democrat, I get to say the committee is in recess.

Attorney General RENO. Thank you.

Senator TORRICELLI. Thank you.

[Recess from 5:16 p.m. to 5:22 p.m.]

Senator SPECTER. Attorney General Reno, I want to come back to the point of how many witnesses there were who testified that hard money was discussed in the meeting attended by the Vice President on November 21, 1995. I want to come back to the point about the available evidence.

Now, it is certainly true that because four witnesses can provide evidence that hard money was discussed, it does not establish with mathematical certainty that the Vice President knew hard money was discussed, but it is pretty strong evidence. And you had discounted what David Strauss had said because, as you put it, he did not recall, but there were contemporaneous notes of his which showed, "35-percent hard, 65-percent soft."

Now, my question: Is not that prior recollection recorded an evidence which could be presented on the issue as to whether the Vice President heard a discussion of hard money?

Attorney General RENO. I do not see how that proves that he heard, that he understood and that he recollected.

Senator SPECTER. Well, that is an interesting observation, but it does not relate to my question.

Let me start again. My question is whether he heard, and then the inference is to whether he knew and understood. But he said that he is an experienced fundraiser, and we know that as a matter of his record. So the question is, when you discount the evidence by saying there are only two of the fifteen attendees who could provide evidence, and you discount Strauss because he has no recollection, I come back again to the point that, as a matter of the law of evidence, that is prior recollection recorded and could come before a grand jury or come before a court probative on the issue as to whether the Vice President heard it; is that not true?

Attorney General RENO. I am sure, sir, that your knowledge of evidence has given you some reason to believe that this could be relevant, and so I will be happy to go back and check it.

Senator SPECTER. Well, there cannot be a conclusive, you cannot mathematically say that the Attorney General is wrong on a judgment call. But I think you can say, as a matter of law, a prior recollection recorded is evidence that could be presented to a grand jury or to a trial court. And the balance of the record shows that there were three witnesses who heard hard money discussed, all of which would have been relevant to whether the Vice President heard it. That, I think, is a matter of law.

Would you care to comment?

Attorney General RENO. Yes, my determination had to be whether the evidence was clear and convincing, and I determined that the evidence was clear and convincing.

I would ask you, if we are all to be judged in terms of whether we are correct or whether we are incorrect by something that happened 2 years before, and we are at a 2-hour meeting, and people talk about a variety of complex subjects, and we are expected to remember or it is to be inferred that we should remember, I do not think is realistic. And, therefore, I found that the evidence was clear and convincing that he did not have the intent to falsely state.

Senator SPECTER. Well, the evidence that you disregarded in coming to that conclusion was one person who heard and another person who could have provided evidence of prior recollection recorded. So that the base of your recitation of facts is erroneous.

But let me move on to the next point, and that is that the independent counsel statute was structured to give the Department of Justice a very limited window on its investigation. You could not use a grand jury to call witnesses, put them under oath.

Attorney General RENO. Could I make one correction to what I believe your point is? You indicated that Mr. Strauss had his recollection refreshed by his notes.

Senator SPECTER. No, I did not say that at all. I said it was prior recollection recorded, which is different from present recollection refreshed. Present recollection refreshed is when somebody looks at his notes, and he remembers. Prior recollection recorded is where someone looks at his notes and says, "I still do not remember—"

Attorney General RENO. But my bottom line is, if the man who made the notes cannot remember, I think the evidence is clear and convincing.

Senator SPECTER. Well, you are at variance with the clearcut established law of evidence that prior recollection recorded is admissible.

Attorney General RENO. Assume for the moment that the fact that he made the notes is evidence that it was discussed, it was clearly discussed according to two people, and the notes indicate that it was discussed. But there are a variety of recollections. Only two people remembered it without having—and even Mr. Bailey concluded that there was a discussion of hard and soft, but he was unclear as to what was involved.

I just do not think, Senator, from a commonsense point of view, that if there was a meeting of this Judiciary Committee 2 years ago, and you spent 2 hours discussing different subjects, that the fact that Senator Grassley said something about hard and soft money that two other members of the committee heard, and one took notes and those notes indicated that that—he verified that that would be his habit to record what he heard, that that would be clear and convincing evidence that Senator Hatch heard or did not hear.

Senator SPECTER. Well, the difficulty with your analysis, Attorney General Reno, is that it is not just those four witnesses. And I pause at some length because an inference is raised that you discount everything you can to come to a conclusion.

Attorney General RENO. No, I looked for everything I could.

Senator SPECTER. Well, it was not a question, it was a comment. And that you leave out Strauss, where as an evidentiary matter he should have been considered, and——

Attorney General RENO. I do not leave him out.

Senator SPECTER. Let me finish now. I will not interrupt you.

And you leave out Bailey, where he should have been included. If you want to comment, you can. I want to move on.

Attorney General RENO. Yes, I would like to comment.

Senator SPECTER. Go ahead.

Attorney General RENO. I did not leave it out. And I would again urge you, as I have urged the whole committee, to read the notification. "While the author of the notes had no specific recollection of the meeting, he did confirm, based on his habit and practice, his beliefs that the words noted in his handwriting were things said during the meeting that he recorded as they were said. Reviewing his notes, this attendee could not recall who might have uttered the words '65-percent soft, 35-percent hard, corporate, or anything over 20K from an individual or hard-money limit 20K' during the meeting. He was also unable to provide an explanation about what each of the phrases might have meant within the context of the meeting."

"He did not recall the issue of hard and soft money being discussed by those attending, but noted that these issues were often discussed at DNC budget meetings. He was also unable to say whether the words were used with regard to the media fund, the DNC's operating budget or something else. Notably, this individual, who attended the meeting and who was paying enough attention to what was being said to take verbatim notes of some points, also told us during his interview that he believed the media campaign was financed entirely with soft money."

Senator SPECTER. Attorney General Reno, I believe the record shows that there were four people in a position to provide evidence. And as your statement said, you focused on only two. But I want to go to the balance of the——

Attorney General RENO. No, sir. I just focused on one of those that you specifically talked about, and I gave you my reasons for concluding that it did not——

Senator SPECTER. Well——

Attorney General RENO [continuing]. Undermine my conclusion that the evidence was clear and convincing.

Senator SPECTER. My reading of the law of evidence is that the testimony that he gave, although not perfect, because most witnesses' testimony is not perfect, would have been admissible and considered by a jury.

But let me ask you about the balance of the witnesses. And I had started to develop the point about the Department of Justice's role at the preliminary inquiry being very limited. You cannot use a grand jury, and you cannot put people under oath. And there is a very big difference between an interview and calling somebody before the grand jury, under oath, and that is not open to the Department of Justice at that stage. But an independent counsel could have done that, so that there might well have been more testimony produced by the individuals if the matter had been pursued.

In regular investigations, the Department of Justice does not stop at just an interview. If they find a witness who does not testify about a recollection or the witness may have the capacity to do so, they use the grand jury. Does the Department not do that?

Attorney General RENO. The Department uses the grand jury in a variety of circumstances.

Senator SPECTER. Well, the point is that your judgment was made at a preliminary stage, where there were investigative tools available, specifically the grand jury, which was not utilized; is that not correct?

Attorney General RENO. I did not use the grand jury, sir.

Senator SPECTER. And then there are the 13 Strauss memoranda.

Attorney General RENO. The Ickes memoranda, sir.

Senator SPECTER. Ickes memoranda. Pardon me. You are right. I misstated that.

There are 13 Ickes——

Attorney General RENO. And there were not 13, about 6 or 7 came before the phone calls, and the others came after.

Senator SPECTER. Okay. You had made that distinction. The FBI report does not make it, but I will accept that.

But if you have six or seven Ickes memoranda, and you have an evidentiary base for the Vice President's secretary, who culls his in box, but who leaves the Ickes memos in the in-box, that raises an inference that the Vice President might have known from the Ickes memoranda that hard money was involved, does it not?

Heather Marabeti testified——

Attorney General RENO. Excuse me just a minute, sir.

Senator SPECTER. "When they, people reviewing his in box, what were they reviewing it for?"

Answer: "They reviewed it for documents that did not need to be in."

Question: "I know that Mr. Ickes sent a lot of internal memorandums. Were his the type of memorandums that needed to be in the inbox?"

Answer: "His were the type of memos that stayed in the in box."

So you have the four people providing evidence as to what happened; you have the Ickes memoranda; you have the Vice President's statements that, although he did not read the memos, as he did a general rule read memos authored by Mr. Ickes, he nonetheless said that, "The subject matter of the memorandums would have already been discussed in his and the President's presence."

And then you have the Vice President's admission about his knowledge of fundraising, that "He had been a candidate for 16 years and thought he had a good understanding of hard/soft money."

So there is an aggregate of information beyond the specific witnesses. Do you care to comment?

Attorney General RENO. Yes. His staff corroborated his statement that he did not, as a matter of practice, read Ickes' memos.

Senator SPECTER. Yes, I know. I just said that. And the Vice President then added to that, that the memorandums, as he put it, had already been discussed in his presence and in the presence of the President.

But let me move on, unless you want to comment further, to——

Attorney General RENO. No. I just want to say, sir, if we get into the business of assuming that people hear something that was said 2 years previously, when there is such a diversity of recollection and where people who, even though they were there, conclude that the only money being sought was soft money, it is going to create a very difficult situation for people in Government.

Senator SPECTER. Well, Attorney General Reno, it is more than a judgment call, it is what I consider to be a misstatement of the facts. But Director Freeh dealt with this directly, and you do not have to agree with him, and the committee does not have to agree with him, unless we think that his basis is correct, and he says, "Based on the facts, the Attorney General simply cannot reach such a conclusion. The evidence tends to show that the Vice President was an active participant in the core group fundraising efforts, that he was informed about the distinction between hard and soft money, and that he generally understood there were legal restrictions against making telephone solicitations from Federal property."

And La Bella said about the same thing, "By routinely embracing the most innocent inference at every turn, even if the inferences are factually indefensible, the memorandum creates an appearance that the Department is straining to avoid the appointment of an independent counsel and foreclose what many would characterize as an impartial review of the allegations."

Do you care to comment?

Attorney General RENO. Yes. As you well know, Director Freeh, and Mr. La Bella and I have some disagreements, as you and I have some disagreements. But I can tell you that this was carefully reached. We reviewed all of the evidence, and we reached the conclusion that we did based on the best judgment we could make. You disagree with my judgment, but that is where we stand.

Senator SPECTER. Let me move on, Attorney General Reno, to the Department of Justice inquiry about the Loral and Hughes matter, about their providing information to the People's Republic of China and a waiver which was signed by the President, notwithstanding that the PRC had sold M–11 missiles to Pakistan which was instrumental in the standoff on the subcontinent between Pakistan and India.

And the Department of Justice had an investigation in process at the time the President was considering the waiver. And Mr. Litt contacted Mr. Ruff, and he testified that he opposed the granting of the waiver and "I said that the judgment of the Department was that it could have an adverse impact, not on the actual conduct of the investigation, but on the jury appeal of any prosecution that might subsequently be brought."

And my question to you is why did not someone of a higher rank, like you or perhaps even the deputy attorney general, weigh in on that important issue?

Attorney General RENO. The White House does not ordinarily consult with the Department on whether to grant waivers permitting the export of dualuse technologies to the PRC.

Senator SPECTER. Well, they listened to the Justice Department on this issue.

Attorney General RENO. May I finish, please?

Senator SPECTER. Sure.

Attorney General RENO. Moreover, the foreign relations issues raised by requested waivers are outside the Department's expertise. When the White House asked whether granting the waiver would impact the criminal case, however, the Department unambiguously responded that granting the waiver would have serious adverse impact if the case went to trial.

As I have testified previously, I believe that I should have been informed. I understand that Bob Litt did not tell either me or Deputy Attorney General Eric Holder about his conversation with Mr. Ruff because there was no disagreement within the Department that the waiver would hurt the criminal case. Still, I believe that Mr. Litt should have told us about the matter.

Senator SPECTER. I do not quite understand that. Was not that this matter of sufficient importance for the Attorney General or at least the Attorney General's deputy?

Attorney General RENO. As I indicated, I was not advised of the matter, and I think I should have been.

Senator SPECTER. You say you were not advised of the matter, but you think you should have been?

Attorney General RENO. Yes, sir, I said that.

Senator SPECTER. Had you known about it, would you have weighed in personally?

Attorney General RENO. It would have depended on the circumstances.

Senator SPECTER. Well, do you know the circumstances?

Attorney General RENO. I do not know what the circumstances would have been if I had been advised of it.

Senator SPECTER. Well, do you now know what the circumstances were at that time?

Attorney General RENO. I do not know what the circumstances were, as they unfolded, or what they would have been if I had been advised.

Senator SPECTER. Attorney General Reno, there have been press reports, the New York Times reported June 23rd, that "The official said that Mr. Conrad had been told to avoid putting his views in writing, and at times felt stymied in his efforts to communicate directly with top officials."

And the Associated Press reported that "It is like a roller derby at Justice. They are slamming him * * *" referring to Conrad "* * * against the boards as hard as they can," the source added. "They are trying to intimidate him to get him to change his views."

Attorney General RENO. I do not think anybody can intimidate Mr. Conrad, sir.

Senator SPECTER. Well, I hope not. Do you intend to look into those reports?

Attorney General RENO. I have talked with Mr. Conrad, and have talked with him to make sure that he is perfectly comfortable, and he said that he was.

Senator SPECTER. With respect to the La Bella memorandum, I understand that Senator Torricelli commented about the timing of it. The second La Bella memorandum was written, I am advised by staff, prior to Mr. Radek's critique.

We are in the last stages of another vote, but let me pick up one final subject with you because I do not want to leave it hanging, and that is the discussion that we had about Mr. Parkinson's memo on the "advice of counsel" defense, and his enumeration of a great many reasons why he thought that the "advice of counsel" defense should not have led you to rule out independent counsel: the absence of direct contact between the lawyers and the principals; the attorneys who gave the advice having an interest; one of the attorneys saying that the advice was "bumping up right against, and perhaps a little bit over, the line"; all of which led him to conclude that the clear and convincing evidence standard was not met and the independent counsel should have been appointed.

Would you care to comment?

Attorney General RENO. Yes, sir. I would refer you to our notification, which sets forth our position with respect to those matters.

Senator SPECTER. Attorney General Reno, thank you very much for coming in today. You are an excellent witness, and you make your case very effectively.

That concludes the hearing.

Attorney General RENO. And you are an excellent Senator, and you make your case very effectively.

[Whereupon, at 5:44 p.m., the committee was adjourned.]

○

CPSIA information can be obtained at www.ICGtesting.com
Printed in the USA
BVOW08s2022011214

377429BV00015B/295/P